THE
GERANIUM
FARM
COOKBOOK

More praise for *The Geranium Farm Cookbook*

"With generous measures of warmth and companionship, this collection of recipes and kitchen wisdom invites us to celebrate the rich flavor of memory, the pleasures of cooking and the goodness of God."

—Palmer T. Jones, director, explorefaith.org

"This cookbook is full of spirituality, great ideas and heart-warming encouragement. So is Barbara Crafton. It is like getting a recipe from a friend while sampling food at a potluck dinner. If you can't get 10,000 people together for a potluck, the next best thing is a virtual potluck-a cookbook. The Geranium Farm Cookbook is a cornucopia of ideas well within the abilities of every cook. If the results aren't always what we want, down on the Farm we just change the name and gussy things up with a sprig of fresh herbs. Farm cooking is all about simple abundance. There are no recipes for caviar in this book. Cooking food is for me one of those deeply healing meditative practices that feed the heart and soul as well as the body. Being a Geranium Farmer is all about connecting with God, the Earth and each other any way you can. Cook, cook, cook! And give the food away if you must."

—Brother Clark Berge, SSF; Society of St. Francis Little Portion Friary; Mt. Sinai, New York

"There is a story of love on every page of this charming book. Each recipe had a history of failure, success, sharing and joy long before it came to be in this book. For just a few moments the reader gets a glimpse of that love. This is a wonderful reminder to those of us who have been cooking day and day out for years or for those who are just beginning their journey of nourishing those who come to them at the end of the day hungry and needing to be loved. Read and use this book and be reminded of love's abundance."

—The Rev. Alice Downs, author, *Leaven For Our Lives: Conversations about Bread, Companionship and Faith-with Recipes*

"It seems the way to a Geranium Farmer's heart is through collecting and sharing treasured recipes. When a recipe is passed on from someone you love, it's like passing on beautiful, tasty fun. Make Cake, or Apricot Sticks, or Whole Wheat Bread for someone you love, then give them The Geranium Farm Cookbook to complete the perfect gift. YUM!"

—Ana Hernandez, chocolatier and author of *Everyday Herbs in Spiritual Life* and *The Sacred Art of Chant*

"Take 10,000 Geranium Farmers who know that eating dessert first is the way of wisdom. Invite them to send in recipes and the memories that go with them. Stir in Barbara Crafton's insightful reflections. Then get cooking! All the makings for a feast of communion, for sharing bread, dessert and life."

—The Rev. Mary C. Earle, author of *Holy Companions, Beginning Again,* and *Broken Body, Healing Spirit*

THE
GERANIUM
FARM
COOKBOOK

BY
BARBARA
CAWTHORNE
CRAFTON

&
10,000
GERANIUM FARMERS

CHURCH PUBLISHING
an imprint of
Church Publishing Incorporated, New York

For Segar Gravatt, genial spirit of the Shrinemont Conference,
whose welcome warms the heart.

Art direction and design: 3+Co. (www.threeandco.com)
Cover photography: Michael Cogliantry

Library of Congress Cataloging-in-Publication Data

Crafton, Barbara Cawthorne.
The geranium farm cookbook / by Barbara Cawthorne Crafton and 10,000 Geranium Farmers.
p. cm.
Includes bibliographical references and index.
ISBN-13: 978-0-89869-508-3 (alk. paper)
ISBN-10: 0-89869-508-2 (alk. paper)
1. Cookery, American. I. Title.
TX715.C8768 2006
641.5'973--dc22

2006016024

Church Publishing Incorporated
445 Fifth Avenue
New York, New York 10016
www.churchpublishing.org

CONTENTS

FOREWORD

Who is a Geranium Farmer?
Anyone who belongs to the easiest community
in the world to join. The Geranium Farm is a
worldwide virtual community of over 10,000
spiritual seekers who choose to begin — or end
— their days with a reading of the Almost-Daily
eMos, meditations sent out into the ether
almost every day by Barbara Cawthorne Crafton.

How does one become a Farmer?
Just sign up for eMos — go to
www.geraniumfarm.org. They'll come
to your inbox until you tell them to stop,
and then they won't come anymore.

How much do the eMos cost?
The eMos are free, always and forever.

*How can I find out what's on the Farm besides
the eMos?*
Well, you could always go there and see.

I mean besides that.
There's a section called "Vigils," in which
you can light a virtual candle for your prayer
intention so that others can pray with you, or
you can chat with other farmers about any
topic you like on the Geranium Farm Bulletin
board. There's a section of links to other cool
websites of a spiritual nature, and a section of
upcoming events all around the country.
There's a bookstore. There's an archive of all
the old eMos, and an opportunity to hear
eMos on audio. There's a section called the
HodgePodge, which has household hints and
stories and recipes and God knows what, and
another one called More or Less Church that
gives people a chance to share creative liturgical
ideas, good sermons, songs, ideas for children's
ministry and much more.

Whose idea was the Geranium Farm?
Barbara Crafton's. She's interested in the
Internet's potential for bringing about
spiritual community in an increasingly
materialistic world.

She must really be good with computers, huh?
Not at all. She can barely press "send." The
Farm's wonderful website is the creation of
Matt the Web Dude, of Big Huge Productions.
Barbara just tells him what she wants and he
makes it happen.

*Whose idea was it to have a Geranium Farm
Cookbook?*
Various farmers wrote in to ask for one. Some of
the eMos have been known to contain recipes
and lore to go with them. Now we have a whole
book of recipes and lore, arranged by category
and, where appropriate, accompanied by a wine
suggestion for each one.

*A wine suggestion? Is Barbara Crafton a wine
expert, too?*
Nope. But Christopher Dole is. He's executive
chef at The Cellar Door, the best restaurant in
Black Mountain, North Carolina. He has kindly
recommended a wine or two to go with each
main dish.

*So is this a recipe book with eMos? Or an eMo
book with recipes?*
The recipes significantly outnumber the eMos
in this book. Farmers from all over the world
have contributed their favorites, and two cool
ladies from North Carolina, Mary Smith and
Heide Kraper, put them together. The contrib-
utors have also provided the lore associated
with each recipe — Barbara Crafton isn't the
only person around here with lore.

EAT DESSERT FIRST

DISCOURAGING CREAM PUFFS

You melt the butter and then you stir in the flour, all at once. Then you break four eggs into this, one at a time, beating furiously each time. The batter gets stiffer and stiffer. It doesn't look like anything that anybody would ever want to eat. It looks like shiny yellow wallpaper paste. Or maybe it looks like latex — yes, I think so. Exactly like latex. *Yum.*

Still you persevere, because your mother told you that it wouldn't look like anything at this stage and you figure she must have had a reason to say that. You drop it by spoonfuls onto a cookie sheet. Or you form it into finger-length strips on a cookie sheet, and then you're making eclairs. Or you make four large flat circles of the batter on two cookie sheets, and that will be the basis for a torte — or four large flat rectangles. There they sit, in their rows on the metal pan: cold lumps of shiny yellow dough you couldn't pay me to eat.

Whatever, you think, *I can always run out to the bakery.* You put the pans into the center of a slow oven and hope for the best. It takes forever. You don't open the oven while you're waiting because your mother said not to and she must have had a reason to say that, although you can't ask her what it was because she died years ago. *That woman is never here when I need her,* you say to yourself. You clean up the disgusting, sticky batter from the saucepan and from the spoon. You put away the bag of flour. Optimistically, you get out some wire racks upon which whatever it is that will emerge from the oven will sit to cool.

At the end of the cooking time, you can look. You roll away the stone from the oven door and look inside. Rows of lovely puffs, high and light and golden and ready to be filed with something wonderful. Or four puffy golden discs or rectangles. What you see in the oven looks nothing at all like what you put in there.

Out and onto the racks to cool completely. If a few dampish filaments of not-quite-cooked dough cling to the inside of a puff when you split it carefully with a sharp, serrated knife, just pull them out and throw them away. That won't happen with the discs or the rectangles — they're thin enough so they always cook through.

There are so many ways in which you can use your puffs: fill them with whipped cream or vanilla cream or with ice cream. Fill them with chocolate mousse. Bury a fresh raspberry in the center of each filled puff. Or surprise people and fill them with deviled ham or crab salad. If you made discs or rectangles, layer them with ice cream or custard into a stack and drizzle melted chocolate over them. Or melted raspberry jam.

Cream puffs are so simple, but they do require faith. You would never continue with them past the first stage if someone you trusted weren't there to tell you not to be discouraged by appearances. Most of us go through an awkward stage ourselves, an era when we so little resemble the beauties we will one day be that only those who love us dearly can make the effort it requires to believe in us.

DISCOURAGING CREAM PUFFS

½ cup unsalted butter
1½ cup white flour
4 large eggs

Preheat oven to 350°F. Melt butter in saucepan over medium heat. Watch it carefully so it doesn't brown. Add flour, all at once, and mix thoroughly over medium heat. Remove from heat and add eggs, one at a time, beating furiously after each addition. Mixture will thicken as you beat it. Drop 3 inches apart onto ungreased baking sheet and bake for 25 minutes or until golden brown. Don't peek before 25 minutes. *My mother said*. Makes 2 dozen small or 18 larger puffs. Or 4 4-inch disks or rectangles.

—Barbara Cawthorne Crafton, The Geranium Farm

LOIS HOOVERMAN'S RHUBARB TORTE

2 cups flour
6 tablespoons butter
2 teaspoons baking powder
2 eggs
4 tablespoons milk
5 cups diced rhubarb
6 ounces strawberry gelatin powder
2 cups sugar
1 cup flour
½ cup butter

Preheat the oven to 350°F. Mix the flour, butter, baking powder, eggs, and milk. Spread the dough in a 9x13-inch baking pan. Place the rhubarb on the dough. Sprinkle the rhubarb with the dry gelatin powder. Mix the sugar, flour, and butter well. Sprinkle the topping over the rhubarb. Bake the torte for 35-45 minutes. Serves 8.

—Chris Jones, Schenectady, New York

CHOCOLATE CHIP–PEANUT BUTTER CHIP COOKIES

1 cup unsalted butter, softened
¼ cup sugar
¼ cup packed brown sugar
1 teaspoon vanilla
½ teaspoon water
2 eggs
2¼ cups white flour
1 teaspoon baking soda
1 teaspoon salt
6 ounces semi-sweet chocolate morsels
6 ounces peanut butter chips

Preheat oven to 375°F. Mix flour, baking soda, and salt together in a small bowl. In a larger bowl, cream butter and sugars until smooth. Add vanilla and water. Add eggs and mix well. Add flour mixture. Mix well. Add chocolate and peanut butter chips. Mix well. Drop by rounded teaspoonful onto cookie sheet and bake 10-12 minutes. Makes 4 dozen.

These once earned me a marriage proposal from a young man dressed in Viking garb, so they must be good!

—Melissa Crandall Everett, Quaker Hill, Connecticut

PRUNE CAKE BY FREDA COKENOUR

(Sounds yucky — tastes heavenly.)

Preheat oven to 350°F. Grease and flour a 9x13-inch baking pan.

Beat 1½ cups sugar and 2 eggs together.

Sift together:
2 cups flour
1 teaspoon baking soda
1 teaspoon cinnamon
1 teaspoon nutmeg
1 teaspoon allspice
1 teaspoon salt

Alternately add sifted dry ingredients with 1 cup buttermilk into the egg mixture.
Then add the following:
1 cup chopped walnuts
1 cup cooked pitted prunes
1 cup vegetable oil
1 teaspoon vanilla

Pour into prepared pan and bake for 35 minutes. While cake is baking, cook in saucepan:
1 cup sugar
½ teaspoon baking soda
1 tablespoon corn syrup
½ cup buttermilk
1 stick butter or margarine

Bring to a boil, remove from heat, and add 1 teaspoon vanilla. Pour over cake as soon as it comes out of the oven. Let cake cool completely before serving. Serves 12.

My grandmother made this for every holiday. I have a complicated family tree — I could compete with the song "I am my own Grandpa." Freda was also my adopted sister and this is her wonderful recipe, given to me on November 4, 1975.

—Linda Pursel, Riverton, Wyoming

GRAPE ICE CREAM

3 eggs
3 cups sugar
juice of 2 oranges
juice of 4 lemons
1 quart grape juice
pinch of salt
1 pint cream
milk

Beat together eggs and sugar. Add juices, salt, cream, and enough milk to fill the freezer. Churn until your arm falls off or plug it in and turn it on. Make ½ gallon.

My grandmother, Mama Bea, was orphaned at a young age and lived with relatives. She married my grandfather, Ted, and moved to Duncan, Oklahoma. After he passed, she married Bill and moved to California where she grew lemons as big as grapefruits and sold her paintings from the yard. Her last years were spent in San Antonio, Texas. She passed at age 97 in early September 2001. She was an artist, like me. This is a secret family recipe, so don't tell my mother, OK?

—Suzanne Armstrong, San Antonio, Texas

CONNIE'S LOW FAT CHEESECAKE

Crust:
24 squares reduced-fat graham crackers, crumbled
⅓ cup reduced-fat margarine
¼ cup sugar

Combine all ingredients and press into the bottom of a springform pan. Chill 30-60 minutes.

Filling:
16 ounces Neufchatel cream cheese, softened
3 eggs, beaten
1 teaspoon real vanilla extract (use more or less to taste)
several drops lemon extract
⅔ cup sugar
½ pints nonfat sour cream

Mix all the ingredients except the sour cream until smooth. Fold in sour cream. Pour into prepared springform pan. Bake at 350°F for 45-60 minutes. Check to see that top is slightly browned and sides have pulled away from edge of pan. Gently touch center; it should be tacky but not liquid. Cool on rack, then refrigerate. Serves 10-12.

Connie was not a wheeler-dealer. She could not charm the spots off a leopard. Her idea of a superb entrée was pork chops fried in bacon drippings with a side order of buttered "Pennsylvania Dutch" style noodles. Although my sister and I doubted that she had somehow coaxed a prominent chef in northern New Jersey out of his secret recipe, we never doubted our taste buds on this one! Very creamy and somewhat less caloric.

—The Rev. Joanna Depue, Orangeburg, New York

MMBJ MOLASSES COOKIES

¾ cup shortening
2 cups white all-purpose flour
1 cup granulated sugar
¼ cup molasses
2 teaspoons baking soda
½ teaspoon salt
½ teaspoon cinnamon
½ teaspoon ginger
½ teaspoon nutmeg
½ teaspoon cloves

Beat ingredients together and roll into balls. Toss and roll balls in separate bowl of sugar. Place balls on a greased cookie sheet and squash each with the bottom of a glass jar. Bake at 325°F for 10-12 minutes. Makes a bunch — 4 to 5 dozen, depending on the size of the balls — and you might want to eat most of them!

Once or twice a year when I was younger, my grandmother would have a special treat for us. The relatively well-to-do family that employed her would produce a bakery box with a couple dozen of the most exquisitely, exotic-smelling molasses cookies, with a granulated sugar topping. The box was very ceremoniously presented to her and she would transport them home by car service and keep them for "a special occasion." The white box with the red and white spiral string would linger in her cupboard for a week or so and tempt us until she could resist our pleas no more.

What a heavenly aroma and taste! For all her glorious baking and delicious down-home cooking, she could not make these cookies herself. About four years ago I recalled those cookies from Mare's house and began searching for the perfect chewy cookies to no avail, until MaryAnn Reed said she thought her daughter-in-law Belinda had one. After several calls from upstate New York to Texas to mid-state New York, a recipe took shape. It was still missing something, so I just changed it a smidge. Since that Christmas, whenever I make these yummies, I can feel Mare passing behind me, reminding me to "leave one for tomorrow, now."

—The Rev. Joanna Depue, Orangeburg, New York

HOLIDAY TIZZIES

½ cup sugar
⅓ cup butter
2 eggs, well beaten
1½ tablespoons sweet milk
1½ cups flour
½ teaspoon salt
4 cups pecans
½ pound candied pineapple
1 pound chopped dates
1 pound candied cherries
½ cup whiskey

Cream butter and sugar. Add eggs and milk. Flour fruit and nuts with half the flour. Add rest of flour to other dry ingredients and mix with egg mixture. Then add floured fruits and whiskey. Drop by teaspoon on greased cookie sheet. Bake in slow oven (300 to 325°F) for 15 to 20 minutes. Makes 5-6 dozen.

—James Ashcraft, Jackson Heights, New York

APRICOT STICKS

1 pound ground, dried apricots
2 cups sugar
¼ cup orange juice
¼ cup chopped or broken nut meats

Combine apricots, sugar, and orange juice and cook over low flame, stirring constantly for ten minutes. Remove from fire, add nut meats and mix thoroughly. Lift small quantity from saucepan with tablespoon. Roll in granulated sugar into sticks and that's it. 2½ dozen.

The above two recipes were my grandmother's, Myrtle Lee Fite, who lived in El Dorado, Kansas. I currently live in Jackson Heights, New York, but am originally from Newton, Iowa, home of Maytag and the "loneliest men in town."

—James Ashcraft, Jackson Heights, New York

FRESH FRUIT TRIFLE

8 ounces cream cheese
1 cup confectioner's sugar
1 cup sour cream
½ teaspoon vanilla extract
¼ teaspoon almond extract
½ pint whipping cream
1 teaspoon vanilla extract
1 tablespoon sugar
1 angel food cake torn into bite size pieces
2 quarts fresh peaches or strawberries sliced thin, or black or red raspberries,
   or blackberries, or blueberries
3 tablespoons sugar
almond extract to taste

In a large bowl, cream together cream cheese and sugar. Add sour cream, vanilla, and almond extracts. In a small bowl, whip the cream, add vanilla and sugar until peaks form. Fold into the cream cheese mixture. Fold in the cake pieces. Combine fruit, sugar, and almond extract. Layer fruit and other mixture, beginning with fruit, in a large glass bowl. Finish with fruit. Cover with plastic wrap and chill well. Makes 16-18 servings.

—June T. Smith, Tuckasegee, North Carolina

HALF MOON COOKIES

(That's what we called them as kids — a.k.a. Baker's Drop Cookies or Half-and-Half Cookies.)

1 cup buttermilk
1 cup sugar
1 cup shortening
1 teaspoon baking powder
1 teaspoon baking soda 1 teaspoon vanilla
2 eggs
1 teaspoon salt
3 cups flour

Cream shortening, sugar, egg, and vanilla. Combine remaining dry ingredients. Mix butter-milk with baking soda. Add alternately with dry ingredients to sugar mixture. Drop by large spoonfuls onto parchment paper on a cookie sheet. Bake at 375°F for 10 minutes. Cool. Frost flat bottom side, half and half with chocolate and vanilla confectioner's sugar glaze icings. Some places put frosting on these, but they really should be glazed! Makes 4 dozen.

Ah...the cookies of our childhood. How well I remember gazing through the glass display at the bakery and trying to decide whether to buy one of these or a large chocolate chip cookie. This one won out a lot and even though I love chocolate, I always liked the vanilla side better. Sometimes I'd even trade halves with someone to have an all vanilla one! It sure brings back some great memories.

—Deborah Sharp Loeb, Freehold, New Jersey

CAKE

(Barbara Crafton notes: *One simply cannot argue with the simplicity of this delicacy's name!*)

6 eggs, room temperature
2 sticks butter
3 cups sugar
3 cups flour
1 cup milk
½ teaspoon baking powder
1 teaspoon vanilla
1 teaspoon almond flavoring

Pre-heat oven to 350°F. Cream butter and sugar. Add eggs one at a time, mixing after each one (do not add all at once). Add flour and milk (alternating, starting with dry and ending with dry). Add baking powder and flavorings. Mix for 5 minutes. You can use a tube pan or a bundt pan. Bake for one hour (please check; you may need to bake longer). Serves 12.

I have been making this cake for 36 years. I got this recipe from a co-worker; it was her grandmother's. When I make it I think of her.

—Gail Myers, Fayetteville, Georgia

GIC'S CHOCOLATE BREAD PUDDING

Take your old bread, rolls, whatever, and soak them in a mixture of milk, a couple of beaten eggs, a half cup or cup of sugar (you can mix the liquids to taste), and a couple of squares of melted baker's chocolate. Add vanilla, rum, or almond extract. When the bread is nice and squishy, bake till the whole thing is set and firm. (About 325°F.)

It needs what Gic called hard sauce. Mix confectioner's sugar with a small amount of milk and vanilla and a dab of butter if you like. This sauce should not be runny, but mound on the pudding where the spoon drops it. But if you put in too much milk, it's still good. Serves 8-10, depending on a *lot* of things.

I don't think anyone would eat it at present, but it's always been a prime favorite here. This of course derives from Vermont where you didn't waste anything, but it may be a bit hard on the birds!

—Betty Rizzo, New Rochelle, New York

COOKIES

(Barbara Crafton notes: *Nor this one! Succinct and to the point.*)

2 eggs, separated; use only whites
¾ cup sugar
½ teaspoon vanilla
6 ounces semi-sweet chocolate bits
1 cup chopped walnuts

Preheat oven to 350°F and center the rack. Spray or line cookie sheets. Beat egg whites until just stiff. Beat sugar in slowly, then vanilla. Stir in chocolate and nuts. Drop batter by the teaspoonful onto cookie sheets. Put cookie sheets in the preheated oven, quickly close door and turn oven off. Do not open door for *8 hours* or overnight! Makes 2 dozen.

These cookies can have a name change to suit all sorts of occasions and messages about waiting, anticipation, etc. They are fun for overnights and retreats and adults get into the spirit of wondering "how the cookies are doing" as well as kids.

—Mary Jane Herron, Woodcliff Lake, New Jersey

PRIZE-WINNING CHOCOLATE CAKE

Mix in a large bowl:
2 cups sugar
¾ cup cocoa
¾ cup shortening

Pour **1 cup of hot water** over this mixture and mix well.

Add:
2 cups sifted flour
2 whole eggs

Beat together and mix well.

Add:
1 cup buttermilk or sour milk into which **2 teaspoons of baking soda** have been dissolved, and mix well.

Add:
1 teaspoon vanilla
pinch of salt

Bake at 350°F in a greased and floured 9x13x2-inch pan for 45 minutes, or in 2 9-inch layer cake pans for 30 minutes. Serves 8-10.

This recipe has been in our family for as long as I can remember (and I am in my fifties now!) and it was obtained from my parents' next-door neighbor when we lived in another state. It has been the traditional recipe for all of our family special occasions, such as birthdays, christenings, etc. When I was in high school I entered it in our county fair as chocolate cupcakes and won a blue ribbon with it.

—Donna Marquardt, Ulster Park, New York

AUNT KAT CAKE

Prepare four round 9x1¹/₄-inch cake pans: grease them with shortening, place circles of parchment paper in the bottoms, and grease again, dusting lightly with flour.

6 egg whites	2½ cups milk
1 teaspoon salt	½ cup shortening
2 cups granulated sugar	½ cup butter
1½ cups powdered sugar	½ cup whipped topping
4½ cups cake flour	4 ounces cream cheese
5 teaspoons baking powder	2 teaspoons vanilla

Have all ingredients at room temperature. Sift the cake flour before measuring, then sift all the dry ingredients together. Cream together the shortening, butter, whipped topping, and cream cheese, until light and fluffy. Reserve 1 cup of the powdered sugar and add the rest with the granulated sugar to the creamed mixture and continue beating until very smooth and light. Add the dry ingredients alternately with milk, folding in by hand, using a large spoon. Add the vanilla and stir; do not beat. Add the 1 cup of powdered sugar to the egg whites and beat with a mixer until stiff. Fold carefully into the cake batter.

Divide the batter among the four pans and bake in a 350°F oven for 30 to 35 minutes, or until done. Cool on racks before frosting. Serves 12-15.

FROSTING FOR AUNT KAT CAKE

3 boxes powdered sugar
1½ cups (3 sticks) butter
1 envelope Dream Whip
4 ounces cream cheese
2 teaspoons vanilla
½ cup boiling water

Have butter and cream cheese at room temperature. Put all ingredients except sugar in a large bowl and pour the boiling water over them. Add the sugar slowly as you beat the frosting. It may not take all the powdered sugar called for.

This is a big, four-layer white cake that is the favorite cake of our whole family, and is made for festive occasions like birthdays, Easter, and sometimes for Christmas. My husband's Aunt Katherine used to make it all the time — no special occasion was necessary. She whipped it up without a second thought, but for the rest of us, it's usually an all-day exercise. But it's well worth the effort.

—The Rev. Paula M. Jackson, Cincinnati, Ohio

FRESH PUMPKIN PIE

1 pie pumpkin (to yield 3 cups pumpkin)
2 cups sugar
2 eggs, separated
3 tablespoons flour
½ stick butter, melted
2 teaspoons baking powder
2 teaspoons lemon flavoring

Cut the pie pumpkin in half. Scoop out the seeds and strings. Place each half upside-down on a foil-covered cookie sheet. Crimp the edges to keep the juice from running over. Bake at 325°F for about an hour, depending upon the size of the pumpkin, until the pulp is soft. Scoop out the pulp and mash in a mixer, blender, or food processor to the consistency of mashed potatoes. Place into a medium-sized bowl. Add melted butter, sugar, baking powder, and flour to the pumpkin. Beat the egg yolks briefly and add to the pumpkin mixture. Add lemon flavoring. Last, beat egg whites to soft peaks and fold into the mixture. Pour into two 8-inch unbaked pastry shells. Bake in pre-heated 350°F oven for 45 minutes. Makes 2 pies; each pie serves 6-8.

Although neither my mother nor my aunt claims to have created this recipe, I have never seen one like it other than in their homes. Don't expect the taste or texture of the usual pie made from canned pumpkin.

—Beverly Jones, Marietta, Georgia

TOMATO SOUP CAKE

This is my family's favorite. It is the holiday cake, the birthday cake, the any-special-event cake. My mother started to make it during World War II and my understanding is that it was developed for wartime use because it needs no eggs, which were hard to get. After all these years (and after Mom is no longer around to ask), I have started to wonder why eggs were hard to get in Brooklyn during the war. Were we waiting till they got rotten and dropping them on Berlin? Maybe it was because the chickens were out on Long Island and there was no gas for trucks to deliver the eggs to the city? Does anyone know?

(Barbara Crafton's note: Most items in short supply during the war were scarce because the military needed them first or because there were fewer civilian workers to produce them, since so many were in the army. In the case of eggs, both these things were true.)

This is not a light, fluffy cake — we like our cakes moist and substantial. It costs a lot to mail a double one, but how can I deny my grandson, now several states away? This is the way my mother wrote down the recipe:

1 can tomato soup
2 cups flour
1 cup raisins
1 cup sugar
½ cup shortening (no rationing anymore — use butter for more flavor!)
1 teaspoon baking soda
1 teaspoon nutmeg
1 teaspoon cinnamon
⅛ teaspoon salt

Cream shortening and sugar. Add soup and other ingredients alternately. Add 1 tablespoon of water to rinse soup can. Put raisins in last. Bake at 350°F in an 8-inch round or square pan or double the recipe for a 9x13-inch pan. Bake until it tests done — when a knife or toothpick inserted in the center comes out clean — try it after 35 minutes. With your favorite cream cheese icing, it is a meal in itself. Serves 8-10.

—Joan Mistretta, Hammondsport, New York

CHERRY VALLEY HERB FARM LAVENDER COOKIES

½ cup butter, softened
1 cup sugar
2 eggs
½ teaspoon vanilla extract
1½ cups flour
1 teaspoon dried lavender blossoms
2 teaspoons baking powder

Cream the butter and sugar until light and fluffy. Beat in the eggs, vanilla, and lavender, mixing well. Combine flour and baking powder and add to the batter, stirring until well blended. Drop by teaspoons onto an ungreased baking sheet. Bake at 375°F for 8-10 minutes until lightly browned on the edges. Cool on the baking sheet for 2 minutes and transfer to rack to finish cooling. Makes 3 dozen.

Frosting:
Put some milk or cream in a saucepan and bring to a bare simmer. Take off the heat and add a handful of dried lavender blossoms. Let steep until cool. Strain out the flowers and then add powdered sugar until a stiff frosting is formed. Frost cookies, and if lavender is in season, add a fresh colorful sprig right on top of each cookie. Definitely for the ladies — do not try to give to teenage boys!

I currently own an herb farm, Cherry Valley Herb Farm to be exact, and have raised lavender for many years. We have an Herb Festival coming up next weekend, as a matter of fact, featuring the herb of the year — garlic. But the recipe here is for lavender cookies, from a few years ago when the herb of the year was lavender.

I also have been lucky enough to travel extensively, enjoying lavender in Italy, France, and other countries — but it was in Taizé last summer that God slammed this 50-year-old between the eyes with an unmistakable message to go forward with steps toward the priesthood. The lavender outside the church and in the healing gardens of the brothers was my comfort as I sat up alone at night, mostly hyperventilating!

Please enjoy this recipe — and many thanks for all the comfort your writings have made at this alarming and exciting time in my life.

—Susan Carpenter, Glocester, Rhode Island
www.cherryvalleyherbfarm.com

GINGERBREAD

(Doubling recommended; both dough and cookies freeze well.)

Mix:
⅓ cup oil
1 cup brown sugar, packed
1½ cups molasses

Add a little less than ⅔ cup water (I shake the water inside the molasses jar to get the last bit).

Sift together and then add to the above mixture:
6 cups flour, more if humid
2 teaspoons soda
1 teaspoon salt
1 teaspoon allspice
1 teaspoon ginger
1 teaspoon cloves
1 teaspoon cinnamon

Chill dough, roll out on floured surface or between sheets of waxed paper, cut and bake at 350°F for 12-14 minutes on lightly greased baking sheet. Touch lightly and when no imprint remains, they are done. Makes 2-3 dozen, depending on size of cookie.

—Barbara Allen, Atlanta, Georgia, author of *Still Christian After All These Years*
available from *www.geraniumfarm.org* and *www.churchpublishing.org*

SUGAR FREE BANANA PUDDING

4 or 5 bananas
1 large box sugar-free vanilla instant pudding mix
2 boxes sugar-free vanilla wafers
½ cup sugar substitute
3 tablespoons all purpose flour
dash salt
egg substitute to equal 4 eggs
2 cups skim milk
½ teaspoon vanilla
16 ounces whipped dessert topping

Make instant pudding according to box directions. Allow to set. Layer one-third of the pudding, banana slices, and wafers. In double boiler, combine all dry ingredients, egg substitute, and vanilla. Add milk; heat until thick. Pour one-third over first layer and repeat layers, 2 more times. Top with whipped topping. Serve warm or cold. Pineapple may be substituted for bananas. Serves 10-12.

My husband is diabetic so we look for ways to allow him variety. My daughter, Kyrah, brought us this one.

—Sharon Marable, Tuscaloosa, Alabama

NANA'S GINGER SUGAR COOKIES

2 cups all-purpose flour
2 teaspoons baking soda
1 teaspoon cinnamon
1 teaspoon cloves
2 teaspoons ginger
¼ teaspoon salt
¾ cup butter
1⅓ cups sugar
¼ cup light molasses
1 egg
½ cup raisins (optional)

Preheat oven to 375°F. Combine first six dry ingredients thoroughly. In an electric mixer, cream butter and 1 cup sugar until fluffy. Blend in molasses and egg. Mix in dry ingredients, then raisins. Chill for 1 hour. Form rounded tablespoons of dough into balls and roll in remaining ⅓ cup sugar. Place 2 inches apart on greased cookie sheets. Bake 8-10 minutes. Makes 3 dozen.

This is my favorite recipe from my paternal grandmother. She was a gentle lady with a wide range of interests and generous presence which invited confidence and trust.

This poem, by an unknown author, was sent to me by my father at a very difficult time in my life. It sustained me then as it does now, as I envision a compassionate God, watching us struggle to weave our lives in the pattern of His call.

PATTERN

If God—or providence, or what you will—
Should, in a laughing moment, turn his gaze
On earth and trace the intertwining threads
We thrust with nervous fingers through the warp;
If he should feel the curious fabric which we weave
With all the alien threads we touch;
Think you that He would frowningly
Deliver verdict: "Right" or "Wrong"?
Or, fingering the twisted strands would He
Be puzzled at the little knots, frayed fringe,
The tight-pulled loops and desperate overcasts,
And wonder if we humans ever guessed
The pattern of the whole?

—Debbie Hickson, Encinitas, California

GOLDA'S KOLACHY

Dough:

1 cup milk, scalded

1½ tablespoons sugar

1 teaspoon salt

1 heaping tablespoon shortening

1 package yeast

½ stick butter

¼ cup lukewarm water

1 egg, well beaten

3½ cups flour

Put sugar, salt, shortening, and butter in a bowl. Pour scalded milk over this mixture. Dissolve the yeast in the lukewarm water. When the milk mixture has cooled to lukewarm, add the yeast and water. Add the beaten egg and some flour. Add the flour about a half cup at a time, beating as you go. Beat the mixture until a spongy mass is formed. Leave this to rise in a warm place until twice its size. Punch down, beat again, let rise again. Punch down, form into small circular rolls. Make an indentation in the center. Let rise again. Then fill the middle with prepared fruit filling (see below) and cover with *sposika* (sugar topping — see below). Makes 4 dozen.

Preheat oven to 450°F; bake until light brown, about 15-20 minutes.

Fruit filling:

You can cook the fruit the day before. For apricots, soak dried apricots for awhile and then cook very slowly, as they burn easily. When tender, beat until smooth and sweeten to taste. For fresh fruit, such as blueberries or blackberries, add a little water to washed fresh fruit and cook very slowly. When the fruit begins to cook, beat and sweeten to taste.

Sposika (sugar topping):

3 scoops sugar

3 scoops flour

½ stick butter, melted

Mix sugar and flour. Pour the butter very slowly into the mix, beating with a fork. This will make little sugar balls.

"¡Buena suerte!" (The recipe card in Golda's hand from which I am transcribing these instructions ends with these wishes for good luck in Spanish. San Antonio, where Golda lived almost all of her married life, is a bilingual-bicultural city where Scots-Irish women learn Czech recipes and speak Spanish.)

My grandmother, Golda Willis Kopecky, was raised in north Texas. Her family was Scots-Irish and had a strong streak of independence and care for the underdog. They were Union sympathizers in a Confederate state. A strong woman with a good dose of the Celtic "gift of the Sight," she went to Galveston around the turn of the twentieth century and started studying to become a registered nurse. She soon met and fell in love with a young physician, Joseph Kopecky. His parents were Czech immigrants who had come to the Czech colony in south Texas. They had a clandestine courtship, for if they'd been found out she would have been expelled. When they married, Golda became a member of a very large, expressive, extended clan of Czechs. Though she never learned the words and syntax of the Czech language, she learned the language of Czech food. For us grandchildren, there was nothing as savory as her kolaches, fresh from the oven, redolent with yeast and fruit or sausage. Getting this recipe out of her before I married in 1971 took some doing. She was a cook who baked by heft and feel, so all of the measurements had to be taken after she'd eyed the amount of flour or sugar or baking powder that she had spooned up for the kolaches. They were one of her many ways of making family communion; we make them mostly for holidays because they are an all-day labor of love; they take three rises. The kolaches are definitely worth the effort.

—The Rev. Mary C. Earle, author of
Holy Companions, Beginning Again and *Broken Body, Healing Spirit,*
all available from www.geraniumfarm.org and www.morehousepublishing.org

PIE. BENEATH THE SKY. RIGHT NOW.

"Wait a minute," I told Norah. "I need to give you some pie before you leave."

I made two pies the other day: one with the last of the rhubarb from the garden, and an apple pie. Like a spawning salmon swimming desperately upstream, I have an inner switch that something in the arrival of autumn trips: autumn makes me want to bake pies. Lots of pies. I bake three, at least, for Thanksgiving. And I bake warm-up pumpkin pies beforehand. Pies for the Christmas Fair across the street. *Tartes tatins*, displayed on lace paper doilies that I hope look French. Lemon tarts. Pecan pies. Pies with different kinds of crusts, just to try them.

Here is the thing about pies, though: in order not to utterly cancel out all my good work pushing and pulling and gyrating at Curves, I can't just go home and eat a pie. So I have a rule: I can eat a piece of pie. That's it.

But Q can't eat a whole pie, either. I mean, I suppose he could, but lately he has taken to referring to his belly as "the corporation." He doesn't want too much growth there. So Q can eat *some* pie, but not a whole pie minus one piece.

This means that people who come to our house often have to leave with pie. It's best if I get rid of about half, including the one piece that is my honorarium for baking the pie.

"That looks wonderful," Norah says, as I cut off a quarter of a ten-inch apple pie.

"That's an awful lot, though."

"We have no choice," I answer firmly, slipping it into a recycled foil pan and shoving it at her. "It can't stay here."

It's *making* the pies that's the most fun. Many times, I have made a pie without eating any of it at all, and it was delightful and utterly guilt-free. Once, I FedExed a blueberry pie to Generva. I forget why.

Sometimes I think that the foods to which we are addicted are only stand-ins for the fellowship we love and crave. Our earliest relating revolves around food — in infancy. We enjoy the material gifts of life first in the company of someone we love. Even after she is gone forever, we can have a taste that reminds us of when she was here. Comfort food, we call it.

But what if we go straight for the comfort instead? What if we delight in the very making of a pie, in the giving of it? What if we delight in the sharing of tea and laughter — mightn't we emerge with such satisfaction that we won't really mind not having had the pie that might have gone with it? What if we call someone we love and have a sweet talk instead of a sweet roll? Or a lovely scented bath with a favorite radio show, instead of a candy bar or a martini? What if it turns out that the things we put in our mouths are all substitutes for love, and we could go directly to love, instead of stopping in first with them?

Just an idea. Here's the recipe for apple pie. I don't measure, but these are good guesses.

APPLE PIE

Crust:

2 cups flour

(You might want to make half a cup of it whole wheat.)

⅔ cup shortening

(Vegetable shortening isn't really the nutritional bargain we've thought it was. It has no cholesterol, but it's hydrogenated, and that's not good. So you can use butter with a clear conscience. I used lard the other day, just like my grandmother did. Sometimes I use vegetable oil, which is virtuous indeed. The crust is tougher, though.)

A pinch of salt

(I don't use this. But most recipes say you should. I don't know why.)

A little sugar

(Sometimes I do this. Sometimes I don't. The crust browns a little better if you do.)

You can put these in the food processor and pulse them a dozen times or so, until the mixture looks like coarse meal. Don't go overboard. If you don't have a food processor, use a pastry cutter, which looks like...well, it doesn't look like anything else but what it is. Find someone old and ask her to show you one and how to use it. You can also use two knives. The old person you find will probably know about that, too. My grandmother did.

Add some ice water. Maybe a little less than ½ cup. Pulse it again, until it forms a ball. If you have no food processor, just stir it around and around the bowl with a fork until it forms the ball. Same thing. No ball is forming? Add more water, but very sparingly.

Divide the dough in half. Dump a cup of flour on a clean surface and spread it around. Take one half of the dough ball and place it in the center of the floury surface. Squash it a little with your flat hand. Roll it out with a rolling pin (rub flour on the rolling pin so it won't stick) so that it's about an inch larger than your pie tin — which probably is not tin any more — is wide. No rolling pin? You can use a smooth large jar or a large plastic soft drink bottle. Then fold the rolled dough up, working from one edge. You may need to ask the old person to show you this. It's a little hard to put into words. You can also say the hell with it and just press the dough into your pie tin. Who cares?

Turn the oven on to 450°F.

Now get some apples, core them, peel them, and slice them in ½-inch slices. You might want to ask the old person about coring apples — if you don't have an apple corer, you can just quarter them and easily dig out the seeds. If peeling the apples is hard for you, just do it for twenty years and it will become much easier. Pile the slices in the pie tin. It should be filled, with the slices mounding in the center.

Mix some sugar — maybe a cup, maybe a little more — and some flour, maybe 3 tablespoons, in a small bowl. Add some cinnamon. Maybe a tablespoon. Whatever. You could add some walnuts and some raisins if you wanted to, or if you suddenly felt it looked a little skimpy. Or don't. Up to you.

Find some butter or margarine. Maybe two tablespoons. Cut it in little pieces and dot them around on top of the apples — evenly, but don't obsess about it. It's going to melt anyway. You could use vegetable oil for this. It won't taste exactly the same, but it'll be good.

Do the same thing with the other half of the piecrust dough that you did before, whatever it was. If what you did was press it into the tin, you can't do that on top of a pile of apples. But you could roll it into long snakelike rolls, a little at a time, and weave them on top of the pie for a lattice top. If you roll it out, roll it up as before and place it over the apples. Cut a few slits into the top, for steam to escape so your pie doesn't explode. Go around the edges of the pie tin and pinch the edges of the crust together. Have your old person show you pretty ways to do this if you think someone else may actually see the pie.

Put the pie in the center of the hot oven. Leave it there for ten minutes, then turn the oven down to 350°F and leave it there some more. Take a look at it after another 30 minutes. If it's brown on the edges and the filling is bubbling a little through the slits, it's done. If it's brown only on one side, your oven heats unevenly. That's not the end of the world. Just turn the pie around. If it's not brown at all yet, leave it there for a few minutes and check it again.

Take it out and cool it on a rack. Or not on a rack. I don't care where you cool it. Serves 6-8. *Bon appetit.*

—Barbara Cawthorne Crafton, The Geranium Farm

PINE BARK

35 saltine crackers
1 cup butter
1 cup packed light brown sugar
½ teaspoon almond extract
5 4-ounce milk chocolate bars, broken into pieces

Preheat oven to 400°F. Line a 10x15x1-inch jelly roll pan with aluminum foil. Lightly spray foil with a non-stick cooking spray. Place saltine crackers, salty side up, in prepared pan. In a saucepan, boil butter and sugar for 2 to 3 minutes, stirring constantly. Remove from heat and stir in almond extract. Pour mixture over crackers and bake for 4 to 6 minutes. Remove from oven, top with candy bars, and spread evenly as chocolate begins to melt. Cool slightly and transfer onto waxed paper. Allow to cool completely. Makes 35.

PECAN PIE

Crust:
1 cup flour
salt to taste
5 tablespoons unsweetened butter
a little cold water

Filling:
1-2 cups pecans
3 eggs, slightly beaten
2 cups brown sugar (half light/half dark)
1 teaspoon vanilla
¼ cup milk
4 tablespoons butter, melted
1 unbaked 9-inch pie shell

Mix filling ingredients together. Add 1-2 cups pecans. Pour into one unbaked pie shell. Bake for 55 minutes at 350°F. This is one of the few recipes that as long as the oven is accurate, bake for only 55 minutes. It's always done. Let cool before slicing. Serves 6-8.

I was given this recipe while in college. The woman who gave it to me said, "Honey, it's really brown sugar pie with pecans, but guaranteed, any man will love it and you." She was right. It is my husband's all-time favorite pie and has been since our college days.

—Aleta Shipley, New York, New York

FLAN: PALANCA

8 eggs
two 14-ounce cans sweet condensed milk
two 12-ounce cans evaporated milk
2 teaspoons vanilla
pinch of salt
1½ cups sugar

Beat eggs with milk; add vanilla and salt. Caramelize sugar in small sauce pan — it should be light brown in color when done. Pour into baking mold and swirl around with wooden spoon until all sides are coated. Let cool. Place a pan of hot water in preheated oven 325°F. Pour egg mixture through a strainer into baking mold, cover tightly with foil and place in the pan of hot water. Bake for 1 hour. The flan is done when a knife inserted in the center comes out clean. Let cool and refrigerate. When ready to serve, invert onto a serving dish. Serves 8-10.

This recipe was given to me by my dear friend, Marcia. Marcia and I shared our first Cursillo experience together and we became good friends. Over the years, Marcia palanca-ed each Cursillo weekend, both men's and women's, with flan to complement the Friday noon meal. Marcia never sought kudos for herself and few knew of her gift. I have shared this recipe with many over the years and I am positive that Marcia would be delighted to have it included in your cookbook. Marcia died several years ago of brain cancer but she has forever left her servant's mark on everyone who knew her. Enjoy!

—The Rev. Nancy Sinclair, Fountain Valley, California

JONATHAN EDWARDS'S CHOCOLATE CREAM PIE

3 squares Baker's unsweetened chocolate
2½ cups milk, in all
1 cup sugar
5 level tablespoons flour or 3 rounded tablespoons cornstarch
½ scant teaspoon salt
2 egg yolks, slightly beaten with fork
2 tablespoons butter
1 teaspoon vanilla
1 baked 9-inch pie shell
2 egg whites
4 tablespoons sugar

Heat milk and chocolate in double boiler or heavy pan. When chocolate is melted, beat until blended. Combine sugar, flour, salt, and one-fourth of milk together. Add egg yolks and blend. Pour into scalded milk; thicken. Remove from heat. Add butter and vanilla. Cool.

Meringue:
Beat egg whites until stiff. Add sugar gradually. Beat until it stands in peaks. Pile lightly on filling. Bake at 350°F for 15 minutes or until browned. Serves 6-8.

Jonathan Edwards was the most famous preacher of eighteenth-century America. He seems not to have been an easy person; he had repeated scuffles with congregations he deemed insufficiently rigorous in the faith, and his most famous sermon is entitled "Sinners in the Hands of an Angry God."

Genevra Miller is a direct descendant of Jonathan Edwards. She contributed this recipe for chocolate pie, which she got from her mother, who had it forever. If she really had it forever, then it must be true that Jonathan Edwards's mother and then his wife made this very same chocolate pie, no? Perhaps Uncle Jonathan's sermons would have been more upbeat if he had eaten more of it.

—Genevra Miller, Wellsville, New York

SCRIPTURE CAKE

4½ cups I Kings 4:22
1½ cups Judges 5:25b
2 cups Jeremiah 6:20
2 cups I Samuel 30:12
1 cup Numbers 17:8
2 cups Nahum 3:12
2 teaspoons I Samuel 14:25
season to taste with II Chronicles 9:9
6 Jeremiah 17:11
pinch Leviticus 2:13
½ cup Judges 4:19
2 teaspoons Amos 4:5

Follow salesman's recipe for making a good boy in Proverbs 23:14. Bake in a tube or bundt pan at 350°F until tester comes out clean, about 45 minutes. Serves 12.

This is intended to be used with the King James Version of the Bible.

—Barbara Mann, Charleston, South Carolina

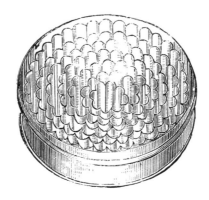

FLUFFY DIP

2 packages vanilla instant pudding
1 cup whole milk
1 cup amaretto
16 ounces whipped topping

Mix and chill. Serve with fruit. Makes enough dip for at least a quart of fruit slices or berries.

—Sharon Marable, Tuscaloosa, Alabama

OATMEAL COOKIES

1 cup shortening
1 cup sugar
½ cup molasses
2 eggs
¼ cup milk
2 cups flour
2 teaspoons cinnamon
¼ teaspoon ground cloves
1 teaspoon nutmeg
½ teaspoon baking soda
¼ teaspoon salt
1 cup raisins
2 cups oatmeal (not instant)

Melt shortening in 3-quart saucepan. (You will mix cookie dough in this pan.) Add sugar and molasses; stir well. Beat in eggs, one at a time. Add milk. Sift flour with spices; add to shortening mixture. Stir in raisins and uncooked oatmeal. Drop by teaspoons onto greased cookie sheet, one inch apart. Bake at 375°F about 12 minutes (cookies should be firm, but not too brown). Remove from pan immediately and cool on a rack. Pour a big glass of cold milk and enjoy. Makes 4 dozen.

—Jane Wacaster, Meridian, Mississippi

EASY GOURMET CHOCOLATE PIE

11½ ounces chocolate chips (reserve a few for the top if you like)
8 ounces whipped topping
1 chocolate graham cracker pie shell
topping of your choice

In a large bowl, melt chocolate chips in the microwave. Start by heating them for 1 minute then stir briskly. If more melting is needed, add another 30 seconds. If you overdo them, all is lost. Dump whipped topping in melted chocolate and stir. Immediately pour mixture into pie crust and top however you desire. Freeze for a few hours before eating. Must be eaten within a few days or it begins to get rubbery. Serves 6-8.

—Cam Altee Brown, Jacksonville, Florida

PEACH PIE

7 medium peaches, peeled and sliced
⅔ cup heavy cream
¾ cup sugar
2 tablespoons flour
½ teaspoon cinnamon
3 egg yolks

Combine all ingredients and pour into pre-made pie shell (frozen is easiest). Bake at 400°F for 1 hour. Serves 6-8.

This is the peach pie my mom used to make. She used pre-made frozen crusts, but the filling is to die for. Let it cool so it can set well, but serve warm with really good vanilla ice cream. Need I say more?

—Deborah Sharp Loeb, Freehold, New Jersey

APRIKOTNUSSTARTE

Bake at 350°F for 5-7 minutes in a shallow metal pan:
1 cup whole almonds
1 cup walnut halves
1 cup pecan halves

Blend in a food processor until crumbly:
¼ cup dark brown sugar
6 tablespoons butter
¼ teaspoon nutmeg
¼ teaspoon mace

Add:
1 egg

Pulse until dough forms a ball. Press into 11-inch tart pan (with removable bottom), using a sheet of plastic wrap laid across to help spread evenly (dough is sticky and crust will be thin).

Mix together:
1 cup dark brown sugar
3 eggs
½ cup chopped dried apricots
¼ cup white corn syrup
¼ cup melted butter
2 tablespoons frozen orange juice concentrate
1 tablespoon vanilla extract or orange liqueur
2 tablespoons grated lemon rind
1 tablespoon grated orange rind

Stir in nuts. Spread into crust, distributing nuts and fruit evenly. Bake on lower rack at 350°F for 35-45 minutes, until center is just set. Cool and serve at room temperature with whipped or ice cream. Serves 16. Nice enough for elegant dinner party; simple enough for an autumn picnic.

—The Rev. Kevin Hackett, Cambridge, Massachusetts

LOIS MASON MEMORIAL ADVENT COOKIES

Blend together:
2 cups butter
1 pound confectioner's sugar

Mix in:
2 large eggs, slightly beaten
2 tablespoons cream
juice of 1 large lemon

In a separate bowl, combine:
7 or more cups flour
2 teaspoons baking soda

Cut butter mix into flour mix. Make into 5 dough balls, cover, and refrigerate. Roll out dough between sheets of floured wax paper. Cut with cutter. Sprinkle with purple and blue colored sugar. Place on ungreased cookie sheet and bake at 375°F for 5-6 minutes. Watch carefully so they do not burn. Makes 5-20 dozen!

Lois was a member of Church of Our Savior in Akron, Ohio. She provided the church school with this recipe to make star cut-out cookies for our shut-ins on the first Sunday of Advent. When she died, we added "memorial" to the recipe name. Batches of dough were made the night before by teachers and brought on Sunday morning to roll out and bake. We invited teachers to bring cookie sheets, rolling pins, star cookie cutters, spatulas, and aprons for the students to use.

We placed the cookies on small paper plates, wrapped them with colored plastic food wrap, tied with blue and purple ribbons, attached an Advent greeting signed by parishioners, and delivered to shut-ins after worship.

—Anita Collins, Shipley, Ohio

McCREA FAMILY SCOTTISH SHORTBREAD

1 pound butter, softened (not margarine)
1 cup sugar, sifted
4 cups flour, sifted

Put the sugar through a sifter so there isn't the least speck of a lump in it. Work that into the butter until it is creamy. Work flour in, a little at a time. Use a fork to begin with, but when it gets heavy you will have to work it with your fingers. Next, roll it (still by hand) into balls about the size of a walnut and flatten them into rounds right on the ungreased cookie sheet. Take a fork and press the prongs lightly around the edges, or pinch the edges to make them look fancy. Make a slight dent in the middle of each cookie and put some colored shot into it. Now they are ready for the oven, which should be set at 200°F. They bake in 30-35 minutes, but keep watch on them toward the end of baking time as they are not supposed to get brown. Lift them off with a spatula and cool on a rack. Makes 5-6 dozen.

New Year's was always a special occasion in the home where I grew up, as my grandmother, who lived with us, kept some of the customs taught her by her Scottish parents. Baking was important, and always included shortbread. Grandmother never wrote down the recipe, but my great aunt did, and these are the directions of Mrs. James Craig McCrae.

—Mrs. Jean (John) Carson, Hillside, Ohio

BROWNIE PUDDING

1 cup white sugar
1 cup brown sugar
2 teaspoons cornstarch
4 teaspoons cocoa
2½ cups water
¼ teaspoon salt

Mix above ingredients in a saucepan and bring to a boil. Pour into a buttered 8x8-inch cake pan.

Cream:
2 tablespoons shortening
¾ cup sugar
1 square melted chocolate

Add:
½ cup milk
¾ teaspoon vanilla extract
1 cup sifted flour
½ teaspoon salt
2 teaspoons baking powder

Combine until smooth and add 1 cup chopped walnuts. Pour onto sauce and bake at 350°F about 60 minutes. Cool to room temperature and serve with whipped cream or ice cream. Serves 8-10.

—Marcia Walker, Union Bridge, Maryland

DIXIE PECAN PIE

3 eggs, beaten
1 tablespoon sugar
1 tablespoon melted butter
2 tablespoons flour
2 cups dark corn syrup
1 teaspoon vanilla extract
¼ teaspoon salt
1 cup whole pecan meats
1 unbaked 9-inch pie shell

In mixer, combine eggs, sugar, and butter. Beat well. Add remaining ingredients and stir thoroughly. Bake at 375°F for 45-50 minutes, or until knife inserted in the middle comes out clean. Serves 6-8.

My mother-in-law, Ruth Walker, started a radio show in Bradford, Pennsylvania, back in the 1950s. She needed extra money, so being extremely resourceful, she approached the manager of the radio station with her idea for a program that gave household hints, information on the community, inspirational messages, and recipes, etc. The manager thought it was a good idea and told her she could do it if she got all of her own sponsors. She beat the pavement and found several local stores to sponsor her show and thus "What's Cooking with Ruth Walker" was born.

She interviewed local citizens, gave out inspirational messages, talked about all matters of housekeeping, motherhood, health, and community — all of this before Oprah! She typed out all of her shows herself and pinned the papers together with common pins (she must not have had many paper clips!) and tape-recorded her programs. This lovely lady also wrote four cookbooks for her family members, hand-typing them and printing them out on an old mimeograph machine.

She is now deceased and I am in the process of going through all of her notes and programs for a possible little book for our family. The recipes I have included for you are from her shows. Enjoy!

—Marcia Walker, Union Bridge, Maryland

GREEN TOMATO PIE

2 cups green tomatoes
1 cup sugar
2 tablespoons melted butter
¼ teaspoon cinnamon
¼ teaspoon nutmeg
¼ teaspoon salt
¼ teaspoon ginger
2 tablespoons flour
2 pie crusts (store-bought or homemade)

Slice tomatoes and soak in hot water for about 20 minutes. Drain. Combine other ingredients in a small bowl and then mix in the tomatoes. Pour into pie crust and top with second crust. Bake at 450°F for 30-40 minutes or until crust is brown. Serves 6-8.

—Edith Phelps, Dunellen, New Jersey

A POEM ABOUT GREEN TOMATO PIE

Green Tomato Pie incredible
And proved itself quite edible
It should win you an Emma
And solve the dilemma
What to make with that unripe fat vegetable
Topped off with a gob of Cool Whip
T'would make the gourmet's lid flip
And appeal to the taste of the culinary chaste
Like green apples without ere a pip
Ruth baked it and to my delight
T'was to my old eyes quite a sight
With golden brown crust
Made my taster buds lust
And it proved our dessert treat tonight
So thanks for the recipe, friend
Our gratitude's yours without end
We will share it with others
Our sisters and brothers
And perhaps set a green love tomato trend!

—Gordon Price, Dayton, Ohio

BAKING FRIDAY AFTERNOON

I could hardly believe my ears: Rosie *requested* that we bake a pie on Friday afternoon. Always say yes when your teenager wants to do something with you — anything this side of legality. It could be years before it happens again.

But very quickly it became *four* teenagers and *four* pies — two apple and two pecan. I laid out four aprons, immediately rejected for reasons of fashion. But the choice of music was a pleasant surprise — they wanted Frank Sinatra. *He's the best*, Tom said. I didn't know they knew that.

Bowls, pie plates, pastry cutters, spoons, knives, peelers: apples were peeled, cored, and halved, butter and flour whirled in the Cuisinart, eggs were beaten with sugar and corn syrup dribbled in. Two balls of American pie crust were soon chilling in the refrigerator. Four people work fast, and Ellen and Tom seemed experienced at peeling apples, something that slows a lot of people way down. We can put the *paté brisée* in the freezer and maybe shorten the chill time a little, I said, and Madeline patted it into two disks and wrapped them in waxed paper. The kids were puzzled that we were cooking the apples in two large skillets, and that there was only one crust — These are *tartes tatins*, I told them. French. Ugh, don't say that again, Madeline said. You sound like my French teacher. It's the weekend. Well, you're going to like them, I told her. You turn them upside down after you bake them. They're awesome.

Wait and see.

Are you ready to rock and roll, Rose? I asked. Expertly, she floured the countertop and her rolling pin and rolled the pastry out thin and flat, then rolled it back up carefully with a knife blade for transfer to the pie plate, an operation words cannot describe very well: you have to be shown. I'm willing to bet that she's the only person in her high school who knows how to do this. Lots of adults don't know how any more.

Should we arrange the pecans on top or just stir them in, I asked, provoking a firestorm of competing views: *Stir! No, arrange! No way! Stir!* The stir faction won out: the kids were getting tired of cookery, and all the nuts float to the top as the pie bakes anyway.

The kitchen emptied as suddenly as it had filled when the pies went into the oven: out to the compost pile with the apple peels, out to the front porch to look at the rain falling just inches away from their faces, safe and dry under the porch roof.

Silence in the kitchen, rain against the windows, the pies in the oven filling the air with their wonderful smell. Then an announcement: *We're just going to chill on Main Street for a while, Mamo.* And they were gone.

Chill. Okay. Just like the pie dough. Maybe we all have to chill for a while, on our way to becoming what we will become. Rest and wait. And think about what's ahead.

TARTE TATIN

Blend 1¼ cup flour and 7 tablespoons butter, in 1-inch pieces — ten pulses in the Cuisinart, or with two knives, until mixture resembles coarse meal. Add 3 tablespoons ice water and pulse again, until mixture hangs together. Don't let it form a ball. If it won't hang together, add another tablespoon of ice water. Pat into a disk on waxed paper and wrap; chill in refrigerator for at least an hour, or in freezer for a shorter time if you need to cheat.

Core, peel, and quarter six large Granny Smith or other cooking apples. Melt 6 tablespoons butter in large skillet; add apples and 1 cup sugar, and cook over medium heat for fifteen minutes. Then turn heat to high and continue to cook until apples are a lovely brown — don't be afraid of how brown they get. Go to Paris and look in the *patisserie* windows: all the apple tarts are dark brown.

Literally *dump* all the apples into a buttered 9-inch cake pan. Wash the skillet in which you cooked them in hot soapy water right away, if you want to save yourself some work; the stuff is murder once it hardens.

Get out the pastry and roll it between two sheets of wax paper until it's just slightly larger than the cake pan, and carefully peel off the paper. Place dough on top of the apples and tuck it in all around them, so that no apples show. Bake at 425°F for 35 minutes or so: golden crust with brown edges.

Take from oven and put a plate on top of the pan. Invert it immediately — two hands, a potholder in each — and tap the cake pan sharply a few times to loosen the apples before removing it carefully. If any apples remain on the bottom of the cake pan, carefully lift them with a knife and replace them on the tart — you'll see right where they should go, as if they were puzzle pieces. Serves 8. Wash the cake pan right away, too, or you'll regret it sincerely.

Et voila! Tarte Tatin.

—Barbara Cawthorne Crafton, The Geranium Farm

BUTTER TART PAN SQUARES

Crust:
½ cup soft butter
1 cup flour
2 tablespoons white sugar
1 teaspoon baking powder

Mix together well with as few strokes as possible. Press into greased 9x9-inch pan. Bake at 350°F for 15 minutes.

Filling:
¾ cup chopped walnuts
½ cup raisins
2 eggs
1½-2 tablespoons butter, softened
½ cup brown sugar
3 tablespoons corn syrup
1 tablespoon vanilla
½ teaspoon nutmeg

Mix together and spread evenly over crust. Return to oven and bake 20 minutes longer, at 350°F, until golden brown. Cool and cut into squares. Makes 9 3-inch squares.

—Fern St. Clair, Cary, North Carolina

BREAD PUDDING

3½ cups sugar
1 quart milk
1 quart water
12 eggs, beaten
1 teaspoon salt
1 tablespoon vanilla
¾ cup coconut
1 stick butter, melted
6-8 cups French bread cubes (about 2 loaves)

Combine sugar, milk, and water in bowl and mix well. Add eggs, salt, vanilla, coconut, and butter. Mix well. Stir in bread cubes. Let stand until liquid is absorbed. Spoon into two 9x12-inch pans. Bake at 350°F for 35-40 minutes or until pudding rises like a soufflé. Serves 18-20.

Whiskey Sauce:
1 cup sugar
½ cup butter
½ cup half and half
2 tablespoons whiskey

Combine first three ingredients in a heavy saucepan. Bring to a boil over medium heat; reduce heat and simmer 5 minutes. Remove from heat and let cool. Stir in whiskey. Yield: 1½ cups.

—Rachael Taylor, Andalusia, Alabama

OATMEAL CAKE

Topping:
½ cup coconut
½ cup chopped nuts
5 tablespoons butter
½ cup brown sugar
¼ cup milk

Cake:
1½ cups boiling water
1 cup oatmeal
½ cup margarine
1½ cups white sugar
2 eggs
1½ cups flour
1 teaspoon soda
1 teaspoon cinnamon

Pour water over the oatmeal and set aside. Combine remaining cake ingredients and then add oatmeal. Pour into a greased, rectangular pan and bake 1 hour at 350°F. Combine topping ingredients and spread over cake when it comes out of the oven. Serves 10-12.

—Rachael Taylor, Andalusia, Alabama

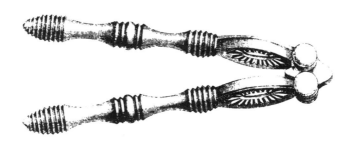

WEEKSVILLE TEA CAKES

3½ cups sifted flour
1 teaspoon baking soda
1 stick butter
½ teaspoon salt
1 cup sugar
2 eggs, beaten
1 teaspoon vanilla extract
½ cup freshly ground nutmeg (or mace)
½ cup sour cream (or ¼ cup plus 2 tablespoons buttermilk)

Sift together flour, soda, and salt and set aside. In a large bowl, cream the butter and sugar until light and fluffy. Add eggs, vanilla, and nutmeg and mix well. Alternately add flour mixture and sour cream to the bowl and beat with a wooden spoon until smooth. Have ready two ungreased baking sheets. Gather the dough into a ball and pat it flat on a floured work surface. Roll it out to a half-inch thickness. Using a 2-inch cookie or biscuit cutter, cut dough into 40-48 circles. Place them 2 inches apart on the baking sheets and bake at 350°F for 12 minutes until lightly browned. Transfer to racks to cool.

Weeksville is composed of four houses on Hunterfly Road in Bedford-Stuyvesant, Brooklyn, New York, which are all that is left of a small but thriving community of free African-Americans who migrated there from the South in the early 1800s. It is now an important historical landmark in New York City. I was privileged, for a time, to be president of the Society for the Preservation of Weeksville and Bedford-Stuyvesant, which restored those houses and got them landmarked.

—JoAnne Williams Carter, Sag Harbor, New York

GLADYS THOMPSON'S PEANUT BUTTER PIE

9-inch unbaked pie shell
3 eggs
½ cup sugar
1 cup light corn syrup
1 teaspoon vanilla extract
¼ teaspoon salt
½ cup peanut butter

Beat eggs well; gradually beat in sugar, mixing well. Add syrup, vanilla, salt, and peanut butter, blending thoroughly. Pour into unbaked pie shell. Bake at 325°F for 40-45 minutes. Top with ice cream or whipped cream. Serves 6-8.

—Charles Scott May, Atlanta, Georgia

CAROL PUTZEL'S CHOCOLATE CHIP PIE

1 cup chocolate chips
1 cup walnuts or pecans
2 eggs, beaten
1 cup sugar
1 stick butter, melted and cooled
½ cup flour
1 teaspoon vanilla
1 9-inch unbaked pie shell

Mix sugar and flour, add eggs then butter. Add pecans, chocolate chips, and vanilla. Pour into unbaked pie shell and bake 30 minutes at 350°F. When finished, it should be chewy, not runny. Serves 8.

—Charles Scott May, Atlanta, Georgia

BETSY'S CHOCOLATE ANGEL PIE

2 egg whites
⅛ teaspoon salt
⅛ teaspoon cream of tartar
½ cup sugar
½ teaspoon vanilla
½ cup finely chopped pecans or walnuts
4 ounces German sweet chocolate
3 tablespoons water
1 teaspoon vanilla
1 cup whipping cream

Beat egg whites with salt and cream of tartar until foamy. Add sugar, 2 tablespoons at a time, beating well after each addition. Then continue beating to very stiff peaks. Fold in vanilla and nuts. Spoon into lightly greased 8-inch pie pan to form nest-like shell; build up sides to half an inch above edge of pan. Bake in a slow oven (300°F) for 50-55 minutes.

Stir chocolate in water over low heat until melted; cool until thickened. Add 1 teaspoon vanilla. Whip cream and fold it into chocolate mixture. Pile into shell. Chill.

—Charles Scott May, Atlanta, Georgia

BUTTERFLY PIES

3 eggs, beaten
⅔ cup sugar
1 cup packed brown sugar
2 tablespoons melted margarine
1 teaspoon vanilla
⅔ cup quick cooking oats
⅔ cup flaked coconut
1 cup raisins
1 cup crushed pineapple (do not drain)

Beat eggs until lemon colored and gradually add sugars, mixing well. Stir in remaining ingredients and pour into two 9-inch pie shells. Bake at 350°F for 50 minutes (or until set). Cool and refrigerate. Best with whipped cream (but then, what isn't?). Each pie serves 8.

—Jane Orenstein, Summerville, South Carolina

GRANDMA'S FROZEN CUSTARD

½ gallon vanilla ice cream
½ cup raisins
½ cup pecans, chopped
¾ cup sherry (no more!)

Soak raisins in sherry overnight. Add nuts and raisins to ice cream. Mix it all up, put back in container, and place in freezer until ready to serve. It's an oldie, but goody! Serves 12-16.

This is a favorite Christmas dessert and a Smithfield, Virginia, must for Thanksgiving and Christmas from my very Southern mother. It's so easy and usually a winner.

—Talmage Bandy, Whispering Pines, North Carolina

MOM'S HOT FUDGE

3 squares baking chocolate
½ cup water
¾ cup sugar
¼ teaspoon salt
4 tablespoons butter
¾ teaspoon vanilla

On a low temperature on the stove, melt the chocolate in the water, using a whisk to mix. Add the sugar and salt, whisking constantly for 5 minutes until the sugar is melted — important to whisk constantly to prevent burning. Add the butter and vanilla, whisking until all is melted and blended. Serve over ice cream or non-dairy frozen dessert on 4-6 sundaes.

—The Rev. Gena D. Adams-Riley and Mary Y. Riley, Pensacola, Florida

SCOTT'S PINCKNEY STREET CHESS PIE

½ cup butter
2 cups packed light brown sugar
4 egg yolks
2 tablespoons flour
1 teaspoon cinnamon
1 teaspoon nutmeg
1 cup cream
½ cup broken pecan meats
1 unbaked 9-inch pie shell

Cream together butter and sugar. Add egg yolks, one at a time. Stir in flour and spices; then add cream and nuts. Fill pie shell and bake at 325°F for 30 minutes or until set. Add brandy if desired. Serves 6-8.

—Charles Scott May, Atlanta, Georgia

SCOTT'S BOSTON PECAN PIE

¼ cup butter
1 cup firmly packed brown sugar
3 eggs
½ cup light corn syrup or molasses
1-1½ cups broken pecans or walnuts
1 teaspoon vanilla or 1 tablespoon rum
½ teaspoon salt
1 unbaked 9-inch pie shell

Bake a prepared pie shell at 450°F for 5-7 minutes. Allow it to cool and reduce oven to 375°F. Cream together butter and sugar; add eggs one at a time and mix well between each addition. Stir in remaining ingredients. Pour into pie shell and bake for 40 minutes or until a knife inserted in the filling comes out clean. Serves 6-8.

—Charles Scott May, Atlanta, Georgia

SCOTT'S MARIETTA LEMON CHESS PIE

2 cups sugar
4 eggs
1 tablespoon flour
1 tablespoon corn meal
¼ cup milk
¼ cup melted butter
¼ cup lemon juice
2 teaspoons grated lemon rind
1 unbaked 9-inch pie shell

Combine sugar and eggs. Add corn meal and flour. Gradually add milk, melted butter, lemon juice, and rind. Pour into unbaked pie shell and bake at 375°F for 45 minutes. Serves 6-8.

—Charles Scott May, Atlanta, Georgia

GINGERBREAD

½ cup oil
1 cup molasses
1 cup boiling water
2 eggs, beaten
½ cup sugar
2½ cups flour
½ teaspoon baking soda
1½ teaspoons baking powder
1 teaspoon salt
1 teaspoon ginger
1 teaspoon cinnamon
¼ teaspoon cloves

Combine dry ingredients. In a separate bowl, combine oil, molasses, and hot water. Stir in dry ingredients, then the eggs. Bake in a shallow pan at 350°F for 40 minutes. Serves 8.

—Rachael Taylor, Andalusia, Alabama

GREAT GREAT GRANDMOTHER DE BEY'S COOKIES {DUTCH SPICE COOKIES}

1 cup sugar
1 cup brown sugar
½ pound softened butter
2 eggs, beaten
2 teaspoons baking soda
1 tablespoon cinnamon
1 teaspoon nutmeg
2 teaspoons vanilla
1 teaspoon salt
3-3½ cups flour
1 cup nuts, chopped

Mix together sugars and butter. Add eggs, soda, salt, and spices; mix well. Add flour and mix well with hands. Shape into two large sausages, wrap in waxed paper, and refrigerate overnight. Slice thin and bake at 375°F until slightly brown, 8-10 minutes. Makes 5-6 dozen.

This is an old recipe from the Dutch side of the family, the one with all the Cornelias! This makes a lot and I think it isn't Christmas without them.

—Cornelia (Corry) Weierbach, Arlington, Virginia

RHUBARB PIE {AS MY MOTHER MADE IT}

3 cups diced rhubarb
1 cup sugar (or ½ cup sugar plus ¼ cup honey)
1 tablespoon flour
1 egg, beaten
¾ teaspoon grated lemon rind
1 tablespoon lemon juice
½ cup water (which I omit in the interest of denser flavor)
1 unbaked 9-inch pie crust

Fill unbaked pie crust with rhubarb. Combine sugar and flour in the top of a double boiler; stir in egg, lemon rind, lemon juice, and water. Cook over boiling water until slightly thickened; pour over the rhubarb and top with a latticework pie crust. Bake in hot oven (425°F) for 40-50 minutes. Serves 6-8.

Everyone knows about rhubarb pie, but who would have thought adding lemony sourness along with the honey would be such an improvement? On top of the latticework, I often add the outline of a heart in tightly furled bakedough, with someone's initials, or Happy Birthday, or whatnot, depending on the season.

—Richard Quaintance, Metuchen, New Jersey

BUTTERMILK COCONUT PIE

3 large eggs
1½ cups sugar
½ cup coconut
½ cup buttermilk
½ cup butter, melted
2 tablespoons flour
1 teaspoon vanilla
1 deep-dish pie crust, unbaked

Blend all ingredients (except crust) and pour into unbaked pie crust. Bake at 350°F for 45 minutes. You may need to cover with foil to prevent over-browning.

—Rachael Taylor, Andalusia, Alabama

MRS. SEYMOUR'S FRUITCAKE

1 pound butter
½ cup honey
2 cups sugar
8 ounces strawberry jam
12 eggs, separated
½ cup grape juice
4 cups flour
½ cup brandy
1 teaspoon cinnamon
1 pound currants
1 teaspoon nutmeg
3 pounds raisins
1 teaspoon allspice
2 pounds mixed candied fruit
½ teaspoon baking soda
1 pound candied cherries
1 teaspoon ginger
1 ounce baking chocolate, melted
2 cups pecan, chopped

Prepare pans: grease lightly, line with brown paper, and grease paper lightly. Makes two large tube pans, three 9x5-inch loaf pans, or four 4x8-inch loaf pans. Use ¼ cup flour to dust fruit. Sift remaining flour with spices. Cream butter and sugar; add egg yolks, honey, and jam. Add flour to the butter mixture alternately with brandy and fruit juice. Fold in floured fruits. In a separate bowl, beat egg whites. Fold into batter. Bake in 250°F oven for 3-4 hours (for a large cake) or about 2 hours for smaller cakes. Place a shallow pan of water in the oven, but remove during the last hour of baking.

This fruitcake can be kept almost indefinitely if wrapped in cheesecloth soaked in brandy and then put in an airtight container in a cool place. A friend told me that she frequently kept the ones we gave her at Christmas until the following Thanksgiving, renewing the brandy from time to time. She then heated it and served it much as you would serve plum pudding, with hard sauce made with rum or brandy.

—Sister Mary Elizabeth, Community of the Holy Spirit, New York, New York

CHET SEYMOUR'S HOMEMADE ICE CREAM

The basic Philadelphia ice cream formula is as follows:
1 quart heavy cream
1 quart milk
2 cups sugar
1 tablespoon pure vanilla extract
dash of salt
any flavorings you care to add
rock salt
ice

Follow instructions with manual or automatic ice cream maker. Use cold ice if you can and use about a cup of rock salt to three cups crushed ice. You can vary the ingredients such as using two quarts of half and half instead of milk and cream. Try buying extracts of peppermint or cinnamon for a refreshing treat. Makes half a gallon.

—Sister Mary Elizabeth, Community of the Holy Spirit, New York, New York

RHUBARB CAKE

½ cup shortening
1½ cups sugar
1 teaspoon vanilla
½ teaspoon salt
1 egg
2 cups sifted flour
1 cup sour milk or buttermilk
1 teaspoon baking soda
2 cups sliced rhubarb

Cream together shortening, sugar, vanilla, and salt. Add egg. Add flour and buttermilk (mixed with soda) alternately. Add sliced rhubarb and sprinkle ½ cup sugar and 1 teaspoon cinnamon over top before baking. Pour into a lightly greased 9x13-inch pan. Bake at 350°F for 45 minutes. Serve plain or with whipped topping or whipped cream. Serves 8-10.

—The Rev. Patricia Guinn, East Aurora, New York

CANDY-CRUST APPLE PIE

5-6 apples
½ cup brown sugar
½ cup white sugar
1 cup flour
½ teaspoon salt
1 stick butter

Slice apples into a buttered pan. Combine remaining ingredients, add a dash of cinnamon and stack over apples. Bake in a 350°F oven for 45 minutes. Serves 6-8.

—Rachael Taylor, Andalusia, Alabama

DEACON'S FAVORITE COFFEE CAKE

3 cups flour
2 cups sugar
5 teaspoons baking powder
2 teaspoons salt
1 stick butter
1½ cups milk
2 eggs

Combine ingredients well and pour into a greased 9x13-inch pan.

Topping:
⅔ cup brown sugar
½ cup flour
1 teaspoon cinnamon (add more if you like)
6 tablespoons butter

Combine sugar, flour, and cinnamon and cut in butter with pastry blender. Sprinkle topping on cake batter and then dip a spoon randomly into the batter to integrate the mixture into cake. Bake at 375°F for 25-30 minutes until golden brown. Serves 10.

—Ken Erb and Anne Lemay, Sewaren, New Jersey

MORE THAN ONE KIND OF SWEET

It's only fair, of course: Anna and Robert have been with us the last two Thanksgivings, so it's definitely his mother's turn. Corinna's new in-laws have invited them and the girls. They've invited Greg, too, and we haven't heard from Sanela — I think she must be having dinner with fellow Bosnian expats. Haven't heard from Rosemary. That's a little odd.

The new in-laws invited us, too. I like them a lot, and they are family now. But it has been something of a shock to give up Thanksgiving as I have known it for so many years: our dining room, so beautiful with the lovely old china and silver, all the faces around the table, Q at the head, carving the bird. To give up the excitement of shopping for it, the early rising to begin making the stuffing, the wonderful smells of cooking that build and tantalize throughout the day.

So somehow I can't bear to go and be part of someone else's crowd. Q and I will visit dear friends in Sag Harbor. It will be just the four of us. Her children are scattered around the country and she is used to not having them on Thanksgiving. I am looking forward to the rapport. To a walk on the beach. We are bringing some pies and some CDs. If I can persuade Q to part with them, we are also bringing some hydrangeas — there are too many in our garden, and now is the time to transplant.

Everything changes. Absolutely everything. We build a hedge around our history with the liturgies of home, with special food, with the sweet sameness of each festival, but it slips away anyhow: you can't hold it.

But you can venture forward into the future with confidence that it will hold its own sweetness; there's more than one kind of sweet.

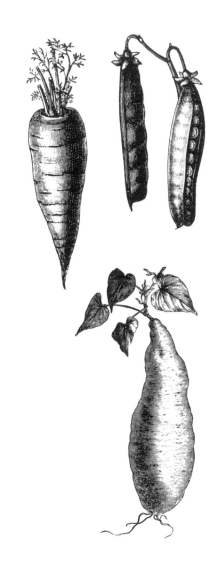

NEW PUMPKIN PECAN CUSTARDS

Delicious, very low in carbohydrates and high in protein and antioxidants. And the nuts give it crunch, so you don't miss a crust.

Preheat over to 350°F.

Whisk together:
2 eggs
1 cup Splenda

Add:
2 teaspoons cinnamon
½ teaspoon ginger
¼ teaspoon powdered cloves

Whisk again. Add:
1 1-pound can plain pumpkin or 1½ cups steamed fresh pumpkin
1 can evaporated milk (fat-free is fine)
and whisk again.

Butter (or spray with oil) 8 custard cups or ramekins. On the bottom of each cup, arrange pecan halves (probably 6 or 8 in each). Divide pumpkin mixture evenly among the eight cups. Place in a baking pan and put in center of oven; add hot water to pan once it's in there to a depth of 1 inch, so that the custards are sitting in a water bath. Bake for about 25-35 minutes, until set: a knife blade stuck into the center of one of the cups comes out clean. Allow to cool and carefully go around edges of each cup with a thin knife blade; place a small plate on top of each cup, grasp the cup and plate together with your oppositional thumbs and fingers, and invert the whole thing. Lift off the cup and there is the custard, standing tall and facing into its future, which does not promise to be a long one.

MAIN DISHES

JOHNNY MARZETTI

6 medium onions, chopped
2 pounds of hamburger (or you can make it without for the vegetarian crowd)
1½ teaspoons salt
1 clove garlic, minced
⅛ teaspoon black pepper
1 cup shredded cheese (or more if you want it; I do!)
1 green pepper, chopped
1½ teaspoons Italian seasoning
1 6-ounce can tomato paste
1 large can crushed tomatoes
2 3-ounce cans mushrooms (or use fresh)
6 cups cooked macaroni

Preheat oven to 325°F. Sauté onions, hamburger, garlic, and green pepper. Add remaining ingredients and cook until bubbly. Add to macaroni and put into greased casserole dish. Bake for 30 minutes. Serves 8-10.

My husband Ed grew up under the watchful eye of his Aunt Jenny, who often made this dish for him. When we married, I wanted the recipe, but it was long gone. Enter my good friend Aline Poythress, the Ragin' Cajun of Port Republic, Virginia, whose mother had told her of this recipe (and eaten lots of it as a college girl!).

And Chris says: *Try an Italian Chianti or Sangiovese to complement this dish.*

—Melissa Crandall Everett, Quaker Hill, Connecticut

UNCLE JACK'S RUSHIN CHICKEN

8 ounces apricot preserves
8 ounces Russian or Catalina dressing
4 boneless, skinless chicken breasts

Put chicken in baking dish. Mix preserves and dressing and pour over chicken. Bake uncovered at 350°F for 45 minutes to 1 hour. Serves 4 if each has a whole chicken breast; 8 if each has a half.

And Chris says: *A French Beaujolais or an American Pinot Noir would work nicely with this.*

—Jack Lowell, Asheville, North Carolina

BAKED ZITI

16 ounces ziti pasta
1 pound lean ground beef or Italian sausage
1 onion, chopped
2 27-ounce cans spaghetti sauce
1½ cups sour cream
6 ounces sliced Provolone
6 ounces grated mozzarella cheese
½ cup Parmesan cheese
2 tablespoons fresh basil, chopped

Cook pasta. Sauté ground beef (or Italian sausage) and onion. Add spaghetti sauce and simmer 5-10 minutes. Preheat oven to 350°F. Place half of the pasta in a large baking dish. Top with layer of Provolone and mozzarella cheeses. Spread half of the spaghetti sauce on top. Then spread on sour cream. Cover with remaining pasta, cheese, then sauce. Sprinkle with Parmesan cheese. Bake at 350°F for 30 minutes. Serves 8 or more, depending upon appetites.

Why it is a favorite: my grandchildren (picky eaters all) love it. It's great for taking to potlucks and is easy to make. You can make it ahead and serve the next day, as well.

And Chris says: *A great paring for a Italian Reserva Chianti, or try an American Zinfandel.*

—Sally Tarasoff, Boerne, Texas

RUSSIAN HAMBURGERS

1½-2 pounds hamburger
4 slices bread, torn up in pieces
½ cup milk poured over bread pieces
½ teaspoon salt
½ teaspoon pepper
1 whole egg
1 box gravy mix or 1 can canned gravy

Soak bread in milk. Add to meat, as well as spices and egg (slightly beaten). Mix well and form into patties. Brown patties in frying pan; then add gravy (should have 2-3 cups) and simmer until done. Serve with mashed potatoes and green beans. Serves about 6.

And Chris says: *American Zinfandel or Australian Shiraz both complement these.*

—Anna Tarasoff, San Diego, California

TURKEY ARTICHOKE CASSEROLE

Sauté in butter:
2 tablespoons chopped bell pepper
2 tablespoons chopped green onion, including tops
¼ cup chopped celery
2 tablespoons chopped onion

Add:
10-ounce can condensed cream of mushroom soup
2 cups sour cream
1 cup grated Parmesan cheese
2-ounce jar chopped pimento
2 tablespoons chopped parsley
dash of Worcestershire sauce
dash of Tabasco
salt and pepper to taste
4½-ounce can sliced mushrooms, drained
14-ounce can artichoke hearts, drained
4 cups cubed cooked turkey

Bake in a 3-quart casserole over a layer of flat noodles at 350°F for about 45 minutes.
Serves 6.

Freezes well. Guys like it even if it is a casserole. Good for pot luck dinners.

And Chris says: *Try an Oregon Pinot Noir or a good French Beaujolais, such as a Morgon or Moulin-a-Vent.*

—Suzanne Armstrong, San Antonio, Texas

CHICKEN ORTEGA

1½ pounds boneless skinless chicken breasts

1 can cream of mushroom soup (I use a fat-free, reduced sodium version)

1 can cream of chicken soup (I use a fat-free, reduced sodium version)

1 cup milk (I use 2% because that's what I have usually)

1 cup chopped onion (yellow, white, or red)

1 7-ounce can diced green chilies

1 14-ounce bottle medium chunky salsa

1 small can of corn, drained

1 pound grated cheese (sharp cheddar is best)

1 bag tortilla chips

Bake chicken in oven in covered dish at 350°F for an hour or until done. Cool and break into pieces. (Or cut into pieces and sauté until done. Or boil it. Or grill it. Whatever, just cook it.) Mix all ingredients except chips and cheese in large bowl. Lightly grease a 9x13-inch pan. Put a layer of chips to cover bottom of pan heavily. Layer half of chicken mixture. Layer half of cheese. Put another layer of chips (both layers are about 2 -3 chips deep). Layer rest of the chicken mixture. Cover and refrigerate over night.

When ready to bake, remove from refrigerator and top with remaining cheese. Bake at 325°F for about an hour or until hot in the middle. Serves 6-8.

The best part is, it really is better if you make it the day ahead and let it sit in the refrigerator overnight before baking. If you don't use the reduced sodium soups, it can be too salty. And, you have to use chips; don't use tortillas. The chips absorb the liquid and make it much better.

If you are cooking for a small family, you can put it into two baking dishes and freeze one before baking and bake later. The cooked left-overs also freeze very well. Get more cheese to put on top when you heat it up. I hate casseroles and I love this. My sister gave me the recipe to feed a crowd of 12 people headed to my 900-square-foot apartment! I made two recipes, I think, and had a bunch left over to freeze.

And Chris says: *Cool this dish down a little with an American or German Riesling.*

—Pamela Leonard, Jackson, Mississippi

COLD SESAME NOODLES

8 ounces Chinese noodles or vermicelli, cooked
1 tablespoon sherry
1½-inch piece of ginger, mashed
1 tablespoon sesame oil
2 tablespoons vinegar
¼-½ teaspoon red pepper flakes
3 tablespoons peanut butter
1 teaspoon honey
ground black pepper
3 tablespoons water
2 cloves garlic, mashed
chopped scallion and shredded cucumber for garnish
2 tablespoons soy sauce
2 tablespoons tahini paste

Add sesame oil to cooked pasta and refrigerate until cold. Combine remaining ingredients; add to noodles. Top with a garnish at the last minute. Serves 4.

Who else should pass on a Chinese/Thai recipe to me than a nice Jewish boy from Brooklyn — who knew? This has been a nice change-of-pace dish in my kitchen since 1988.

And Chris says: *Another good candidate for the American or German Riesling treatment.*

—The Rev. Joanna Depue, Orangeburg, New York

ZUCCHINI CASSEROLE

3 tablespoons butter
2 tablespoons flour
½ teaspoon salt
4 eggs, beaten
½ teaspoon pepper
1 cup sour cream
¼ teaspoon garlic powder
1 pound mushrooms, sliced thin
Italian bread crumbs
1 cup Provolone cheese, grated
1 teaspoon Italian seasoning
6 small or 4 medium zucchini, sliced thin
grated Romano cheese for topping

Sauté zucchini, mushrooms, and seasonings in butter until tender. Add sour cream to beaten eggs, then add flour and Provolone cheese. Add vegetable mixture and turn into baking dish. Sprinkle Romano cheese on top, then cover with Italian bread crumbs. Dot with butter and bake in 350°F oven for 40 minutes. Serves 8.

And Chris says: *American Pinot Gris or Italian Pinot Grigio to complement the zucchini.*

—June T. Smith, Tuckasegee, North Carolina

BRAISED CHICKEN WITH BUTTERNUT SQUASH, WALNUTS, AND SAGE

2 tablespoons olive oil or vegetable oil

3 tablespoons unsalted butter

One 3½-pound chicken, cut into 8 pieces (2 breasts, 2 wings, 2 legs, 2 thighs)

fine sea salt and freshly ground black pepper

½ cup onion, diced

1 carrot, diced

2 cups butternut squash, peeled and cut into 1-inch dice (about 2 pounds squash)

1 tablespoon ground cinnamon

½ teaspoon ground cloves

½ teaspoon ground ginger

1½ cups homemade chicken stock or low-sodium, store-bought chicken broth, simmering in a pot

½ cup finely chopped walnuts, plus more for serving

2 tablespoons chopped sage, plus more for serving

Heat the oil and melt 1 tablespoon of the butter over medium heat. Season the chicken parts generously with salt and pepper. Add the chicken pieces to the pan and cook slowly until golden brown, about 8 minutes. Turn the pieces over and brown the other side, about 8 more minutes. Transfer the chicken pieces to a plate and cover loosely with foil to keep warm. Set aside.

Add the onion, carrots, and squash to the pan and sauté until softened but still holding their shape, 6 to 8 minutes. Stir in the cinnamon, clove, and ginger. Pour in the stock, return the chicken to the pan, raise the heat to high and bring the liquid to a boil. Lower the heat and let simmer until the chicken shows no pink when pierced at the joint, about 20 minutes. Taste the sauce and season it with salt and pepper. Remove the chicken from the pan and arrange the pieces on a serving platter. Add the walnuts and sage leaves to the pan and cook for 2 minutes. Add the remaining 2 tablespoons butter, stirring it in to give the sauce a smooth finish.

Spoon the vegetables around the chicken and pour any extra sauce over the chicken. Sprinkle more sage and walnuts over the dish and serve. Serves 4.

—Gordon Boals, Somerset, New Jersey

MEATLOAF ON TOP OF THE CAR

1 pound ground chuck
cornflakes to feel
egg
salt and pepper
pinch of rosemary
pinch of garlic powder
can of tomato soup

Mix the above ingredients all up and squish together. Pat into loaf.

Sauce:
can of tomato sauce
brown sugar
dark brown mustard

Mix and pour over meatloaf and baste while cooking now and then at 350°F for about an hour. The exact ingredients are not as important as having it sail into a new neighbor's front yard. Serves 4-6.

This is good for meeting your new neighbors. I made this meatloaf when all the kids were little, put it on top of the Chevy wagon so as to get all the kids in place and referee a debate or two, hopped in and drove down the driveway to bake the meatloaf (my oven was broken at the time so was going to my sister-in-law's house). My job there was to baby-sit her five kids and feed them the delicious meatloaf. As I drove down the driveway, the meatloaf sailed off the roof of the car and landed in the new neighbor's front yard. The new neighbor mom, Peggy Garbooshian, looked stunned when the meatloaf landed. After all, it was our first hello. When I scraped up the meatloaf and said my hellos (and goodbyes), this time the meatloaf sitting square on the floor of the car, I knew that Peggy and I had made a good start. Any pretense of the perfect mom, perfect cook stuff was kaput, finished, cooked.

And Chris says: *Go airborne with a nice American Zinfandel; a single vineyard wine would be best.*

—Norah McCormack, Metuchen, New Jersey

NOT MY MOTHER'S POT ROAST

1½ to 2 pounds beef round roast, frozen
4 cloves garlic, minced
1 14½-ounce can beef broth
2 14½-ounce cans chopped tomatoes, undrained
1½ cups cold coffee
1 bay leaf
½ teaspoon French tarragon
2 tablespoons dried porcini mushrooms
1 tablespoon balsamic vinegar
1 tablespoon Worcestershire sauce
5 small yellow onions
Potatoes, carrots, green beans, and/or any other fresh or frozen vegetable that you prefer
½ cup sour cream

Preheat the oven to 500°F. Place the frozen meat in the pot.

Combine all the ingredients, except the sour cream. Add additional liquids (broth and/or coffee) so that the meat is covered. Cover pot and place it in the oven, reducing the heat to 300°F. Add the vegetables to the pot, allowing for their own respective cooking time. When meat is tender, remove it to slice in thick pieces. Return the roast to the oven for another half hour, so that the juices penetrate the meat.

On serving, whisk the sour cream into the juices for a very satisfying gravy. Serves 4-6.

Because of her nursing training, my mother believed in killing bacteria by cooking everything to death. Consequently, she burned beyond recognition the pot roast she thought her son adored. This version of a winter's Sunday dinner begins with frozen meat, which helps the dish retain its moisture. Put it in the oven before you go to church, preferably an Episcopal church. It just makes the roast even better.

And Chris says: *Try an American Merlot or Cabernet Sauvignon, although the Cabernet might have a leg up on this dish.*

—Jeffrey Deutsch, St. Louis, Missouri

GENERAL JANE'S CHICKEN

This is one of those tasty, easy dishes that you can expand or contract without losing the essential flavors. This version serves 4. The idea for it came from trying to concoct something tasty that would pass muster on a Weight Watchers diet. It was named General Jane's Chicken by my son-in-law, who loves to cook. It was only when I saw his recipe card that I found out I'm known as General Jane in that part of the family!

4 chicken breast halves
1 can black beans, partially drained
2-3 ounces grated cheese of your choice, or more
1 8-ounce jar salsa
1 teaspoon cumin
1 teaspoon garlic powder
1 teaspoon chili powder
½ teaspoon salt
½ teaspoon pepper

For the topping: some chopped cilantro if you have it handy, or maybe some black olive pieces or sour cream — none of these are essential. Mix the cumin, garlic powder, chili powder, salt, and pepper. Season the chicken breasts with about half of this mixture and brown them lightly in a frying pan. Drain the beans and mix the rest of the seasoning mix right into the beans in the can. Put the chicken into a casserole, top with the seasoned beans, then the salsa, and top with cheese. Bake for about 30 minutes at 350°F. If desired, before serving sprinkle with some chopped cilantro, black olive pieces, or sour cream for a little extra zip. This recipe works well with fish also. Serves 4.

And Chris says: *If you like white wine, try an American Riesling. Thirsty for red? Try a Spanish Rioja.*

—Jane Graham, Austin, Texas

GREEK-STYLE LEG OF LAMB

My Education for Ministry class uses this recipe for our annual Seder supper main course.

4 pounds boneless, butterflied leg of lamb
½ cup olive oil
½ cup lemon juice
1 tablespoon onion powder
1 tablespoon fresh oregano
2 tablespoons fresh rosemary
6 cloves garlic, crushed

Trim fat from lamb. Place in a large, heavy-duty "zip" plastic bag. Combine oil and remaining 5 ingredients; pour over the lamb. Seal bag. Marinate in refrigerator at least 4 hours, turning occasionally. Remove lamb from marinade, discarding marinade.

Grill, uncovered, over medium coals for 20 minutes. Turn and grill 20 minutes more or until a meat thermometer inserted registers 150-160°F maximum. Let stand 10 minutes. Slice diagonally across the grain. Serves 10-12.

And Chris says: *A classic pairing for French red Bordeaux, and don't bother with the cheap stuff — you won't regret spending a few extra dollars.*

—Lynn Ronkainen, Houston, Texas

SAUCY FISH CAKES

1½ pounds steamed fish
1 potato, mashed
1 diced raw onion
2 tablespoons minced fresh coriander (cilantro)
½ sweet bell pepper, diced
beaten eggs
bread crumbs

Flake the fish in a large mixing bowl. Add the mashed potato — you can leave the skin on the potato, if you are lazy like me. Stir in the raw onion, bell pepper, coriander (cilantro) with salt and pepper to season. Form the mixture into patties. Dip them in the beaten egg, then in the bread crumbs. Fry them in shortening and watch them carefully. They cook up quickly. Serve the fish cakes on a bed of dressed greens with the sauce on each cake. Serves 6.

Sauce:
1 cup mayonnaise
3 heaping tablespoons horseradish
1 teaspoon lemon juice
3 heaping tablespoons taramosalata (Greek fish roe)

(If the taramosalata is not available, substitute 1 tablespoon of anchovy paste.)

And Chris says: *Take your pick: an American Pinot Noir or Chardonnay, or a French Chablis.*

—Jeffrey Deutsch, St. Louis, Missouri

FRESH PASTA WITH LAMB AND ARTICHOKES

2 pounds diced lamb
1 liter white wine
8 chopped onions
dash nutmeg
3 dashes of hot paprika
1 can quartered artichokes
flour
extra virgin olive oil
pasta of choice

Dust the diced lamb with flour and brown the cubes in 2 tablespoons of extra virgin olive oil in a skillet. Add the onions and cover the skillet until the onions sweat. Add the white wine with the juice from the can of artichokes and simmer for a good 3 hours to reduce the sauce, dissolve the onions, and separate the meat.

Add the artichokes to the sauce only at the end to heat the artichoke. Then add fresh pasta of your choice. The broader the noodle, the better the dish. Serves 8-10.

There are only a few ingredients, and the secret of this dish is in the quality of your spices.

And Chris says: *Try putting a bottle of American Viognier in the dish and one or more bottles on the table. If you like red, this dish would be good with a bottle of Viognier in the dish and a young and fruity French red Bordeaux on the table.*

—Jeffrey Deutsch, St. Louis, Missouri

POKE CHOPS

Here is the recipe for a schmear that you put on the chop before the grill or the broil. By the way, this schmear is versatile and works with steaks and chicken, as well.

Combine peanut sauce or smooth peanut butter with a bit of lemon juice and olive oil. Add mustard that has a kick (a Chinese mustard might work). Schmear it on the meat and grill the meat.

And Chris says: *When in doubt — American Zinfandel!*

—Jeffrey Deutsch, St. Louis, Missouri

TOMATO PIE

1 frozen pie shell
4-6 ounces mozzarella cheese
1 medium onion
2 large tomatoes
½ cup heavy cream
1 large egg
½ cup parmesan cheese
1 tablespoon Italian herbs mixed with 1 clove minced garlic
3 tablespoons mustard (not yellow)

Preheat oven to 350°F. Chop onion and sauté in olive oil until very dark, but not burned. Spread mustard over the bottom of the pie shell. Spread onions over the mustard. Chop mozzarella and spread over the onions. Slice tomatoes thinly and place on top of the cheese, overlapping the slices. Mix cream and egg together and pour over the pie. Sprinkle with the parmesan cheese and the herb/garlic mixture. Bake for half an hour or until done. Let rest for 15 minutes before serving. Serve with salad with vinaigrette and a nice wine. Serves 6.

And Chris says: *With this tasty dish, try an Australian Chardonnay or American Viognier.*

—Alice Downs, Atlantic Highlands, New Jersey

FLANK STEAK

¼ cup soy sauce
1 tablespoon minced garlic
3 tablespoons honey
¼ cup sliced scallions
2 tablespoons vinegar
¼ cup olive oil
1 tablespoon minced fresh ginger
1½ pounds flank steak

Combine first 7 ingredients. Add steak and marinate overnight. Broil or grill 5-10 minutes on each side. Slice thinly against the grain. Serves 4.

This is easy, fool-proof, and delicious. It's the first thing my daughters ask for when they come home from school.

And Chris says: *Hmmm...New world, Cabernet Sauvignon; or the old world, an Italian Brunello di Montalcino.*

—Gary Carter, Alexandria, Virginia

KROPSUA

2 cups milk
1 cup flour
3 eggs
3 tablespoons sugar
1 teaspoon salt
¼ cup melted butter

Mix ingredients together well. This makes a thin batter. Grease hot pie pans (or other flat pans) and pour the batter quickly. Bake in a hot oven for about 20 minutes. Serve immediately as they will drop fast. Best with real maple syrup. Yield: 2-3 servings.

This was a favorite Sunday night supper dish recipe given to me by our Swedish "grandma" in Wyoming. She was the old country kind of Swede who would place a sugar lump between her teeth and her cheek as she drank her coffee.

And Chris says: *An American or Spanish sparkling wine goes well with this dish, on its own or as a Champagne cocktail with a twist of orange peel and a teaspoon of brandy in each glass.*

—Nancy Ost, New York, New York

SPINACH CORONA

1 package frozen chopped spinach
2 tablespoons flour (I use whole wheat)
¼ cup melted butter
2 cups cottage cheese
3 eggs
½ teaspoon nutmeg
¾ cup cheddar cheese (or more)

Mix well. Bake at 350°F for 1 hour. As a side dish, this serves 4.

I learned about this very easy and delicious recipe from my daughter Beth in Nashville, Tennessee. Everyone usually enjoys this dish even if they do not think they like spinach.

—Sissie Hodges, Signal Mountain, Tennessee

TAMALE PIE

Pie crust:
4 cups water
1 cup cornmeal
1 teaspoon salt

Bring 3 cups water to a boil. Combine remaining cup with cornmeal and salt. Slowly pour into boiling water, stirring constantly, until thickened. Put lid on pot and simmer for five minutes. Spread about 3/4 of corn meal mush on bottom and sides of 9x12-inch casserole dish. Set remaining mush aside.

Filling:
2 tablespoons oil
1 pound ground chuck or 2 cups shredded, cooked chicken
1 medium yellow onion, chopped
2 cloves garlic, minced
1 heaping teaspoon chili powder
1 can pitted olives
1 large can of tomatoes
4 ounces tomato paste
1 package frozen whole kernel corn
2 tablespoons cilantro, chopped

In skillet, heat oil and sauté onions and garlic until limp and light brown. Add meat, breaking into chunks, and chili powder and cook 10 minutes, or until meat is cooked. Add tomatoes, corn, and olives and simmer 10 minutes, stirring often. Add salt and pepper to taste; stir in cilantro.

Add filling to prepared cornmeal mush. Using a cookie cutter, stamp out shapes from the remaining mush and transfer them to the top of the pie. Decorate with extra olives if you like and sprinkle with paprika and/or grated cheese. Bake at 400°F for 20 minutes. Serves 6-8.

And Chris says: *Try an American Petite Sirah (Syrah) or South American Merlot.*

—Robin Rule, New York, New York

GRANDMOMMIE'S FRIED CHICKEN

Clean chicken by soaking in vinegar and salt water. Remove excess fat, all feathers, and slimy stuff. Pat the chicken dry. Sprinkle with salt, pepper, onion, and garlic powder; then coat with flour. Place coated chicken in very hot oil for 1-2 minutes, and then reduce heat to medium. Fry for about 7-10 minutes on each side (more or less depending on size of the pieces). When done, remove pieces from pan and drain on paper towel.

My mother's chicken is legendary in our family. My son's (sort of) first sentence after eating her chicken was "UMMM goo." And it is! Good luck. This is her recipe, or as near as I can tell. She says the secret to a good fried chicken that is crisp and golden brown on the outside, yet moist on the inside, is making sure the grease (oil) is very hot at first, and then lower it to medium a few moments after adding the chicken. She mostly used a large cast-iron frying pan, though she was successful with any frying pan. Cook like-size pieces together (legs with legs, breasts with breasts, etc.).

And Chris says: *A white wine goes well with chicken. Try Sauvignon Blanc from New Zealand or California or a Gewurztraminer from Alsace.*

—Antoinette Foy, New York, New York

GREEK ISLAND FISH PACKETS

1 medium onion, sliced
1 large green pepper, sliced
1 large zucchini, sliced lengthwise
14-ounce can Italian flavored diced tomatoes, undrained
1 clove garlic, pressed
4 firm white fish fillets
Salt and pepper to taste
Greek seasoning

Put one-quarter of each of the above ingredients on a square of heavy aluminum foil, folding and sealing into a packet that has room for air on top of the packet. Cook on the grill for 18-22 minutes, or in an oven at 400°F for 15-20 minutes. Serves 4.

And Chris says: *An Italian Pinot Grigio or a Washington State Riesling complement this fish entrée.*

—Sissie Hodges, Signal Mountain, Tennessee

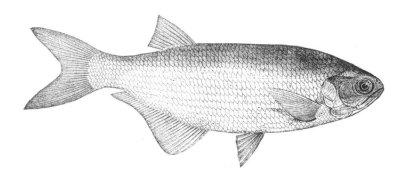

ROAST SALMON WITH CAPERS AND TARRAGON

3 tablespoons butter or margarine
¼ cup plain breadcrumbs
¼ cup loosely packed minced parsley
3 tablespoons drained capers
1 teaspoon dried tarragon or 2 tablespoons fresh tarragon
2 tablespoons grated fresh lemon peel
¼ teaspoon salt
¼ teaspoon pepper
1 whole salmon fillet (2-3 pounds)
lemon wedges and fresh tarragon sprigs for garnish

Preheat oven to 450°F. In a 1-quart saucepan, melt margarine over low heat. Remove saucepan from heat; stir in breadcrumbs, parsley, capers, dried tarragon, lemon peel, salt, and pepper. Line a jelly roll pan with lightly greased foil. Place salmon, dark side down, in pan and pat crumb mixture on top. Roast 30 minutes or until salmon turns opaque throughout and topping is lightly browned. With two large spatulas, carefully transfer salmon to platter. Garnish with lemon wedges and tarragon sprigs. Yield: 4-6 servings.

And Chris says: *A good Oregon or California Pinot Noir, or French Chateauneuf-du-Pape. Your choice!*

—Mooydeen C. Frees, Cincinnati, Ohio

VEGETABLE PIE

1 package frozen broccoli
1 package frozen spinach
10 ounces mushrooms, chopped
1 medium onion, chopped
2 cloves garlic, minced
¼ pound shredded cheese of your choice
1 egg
28-ounce can sweet potatoes in syrup
milk
butter
salt and pepper to taste
2 unbaked 9-inch pie shells

Preheat oven to 375°F. Pierce one of the pie shells all over with a fork. Bake in oven for 10 minutes. Cook spinach and broccoli until done. Drain completely and, when cool enough, squeeze very, very dry. Sauté onion until translucent. Add mushrooms, garlic, salt, and pepper and cook over moderate heat until liquid evaporates. Beat the egg. Mix the broccoli and spinach with the mushroom mixture and when cool, add egg and mix. Cook the sweet potatoes in syrup. When heated through, drain and mix in milk, butter, salt, and pepper; mash. Add the vegetable mixture to the pre-baked pie shell and spread evenly. Place the cheese slices on top of the vegetables. Spread the mashed sweet potatoes on top of the cheese. Cut the second pie shell into strips and make a lattice decoration on top of the pie. Bake for 30-40 minutes.

And Chris says: *Just about anything from the French Alsace region suits this dish perfectly.*

—Vincent Maiolo, Piscataway, New Jersey

SPICY SQUASH CASSEROLE

1 pound yellow squash, sliced
1 pound zucchini, sliced
1 medium onion, chopped
1 tablespoon olive oil
10-ounce can Rotel tomatoes with chilies, drained
1 teaspoon salt
1 cup reduced-fat sharp cheddar cheese, shredded
bread crumbs

Microwave or steam squash until almost tender. Sauté onion in oil; add tomatoes and salt. Put half the squash in 9x13-inch baking dish; add tomato sauce and then the rest of the squash. Sprinkle with cheese and bread crumbs. Bake uncovered at 350°F for 30 minutes. Serves 2-4. Serve with crusty bread.

And Chris says: *I think spicy and I think Washington State Riesling, but if it's not too spicy any young white wine is fine.*

—Becky Kindergan, Pensacola, Florida

LIFFEY SALMON CASSEROLE

3 cups cooked mashed potatoes
10-12 ounces broiled or grilled salmon
3 eggs, beaten
½ cup onions, minced
½ teaspoon pepper
2 medium tomatoes, thinly sliced
8 ounces sharp cheddar, grated
1 tablespoon fresh parsley, chopped
¼ cup dry bread crumbs
¼ cup freshly grated Parmesan cheese

Break the grilled fillets into chunks. In a medium bowl, combine salmon, eggs, onions, and pepper. Pour this into a 7x11-inch baking dish sprayed with cooking spray. Arrange sliced tomatoes over the salmon mixture. Sprinkle with cheese.

Mix the parsley with the prepared mashed potatoes. Spread on top of the salmon and cheese layers in the casserole. Combine the breadcrumbs and Parmesan cheese and sprinkle over potatoes. Bake at 350°F for 30-35 minutes, until potatoes are slightly browned. Serves 6.

I fell in love with fresh salmon on a trip to Ireland many years ago and always associate this dish with the pub grub of Dublin. Thus, I believe it is best to enjoy this casserole with a pint of stout Irish beer.

And Chris says: *Or how about a glass or two of Oregon Pinot Noir?*

—Walt Kindergan, Pensacola, Florida

TWICE-BAKED POTATO CASSEROLE

6 medium unpeeled potatoes, baked
½ teaspoon salt
¼ teaspoon pepper
1 pound sliced bacon, cooked and crumbled
3 cups sour cream (24 ounces total)
2 cups shredded mozzarella cheese
2 green onions, chopped

Cut baked potatoes into 1-inch cubes. Place half in greased 9x13-inch baking dish. Sprinkle with half of the salt, pepper, and bacon. Top with half of sour cream and cheeses. Repeat layers. Bake uncovered at 350°F for 20 minutes, or until cheese is melted. Sprinkle with onions. Serves 6-8.

—Faye Arnold, Dalton, Georgia

CURRIED CELERY SOUP

4 to 8 chopped stalks celery
1 onion, chopped
dash of cabbage, red pepper, garlic, grape leaves (if available)

Cover liberally with several cups of water or chicken broth and spice to taste with curry, basil, ginger, rosemary, sage, and/or thyme. Put in a generous sprinkling of black pepper. Bring to boil, then turn down heat and simmer until vegetables are tender and broth is flavorful.

This delicious soup is also described as a recipe for arthritis relief!

—Patti Bartleson, Atlantic Beach, Florida

SQUASH CASSEROLE

Buy small squash — about 10 of them. Slice and cook with half a small onion you have finely chopped in about a cup of water. When the squash and onion are sort of tender, drain. (I drink the cooking water when I am done with the recipe.) In a separate bowl, scramble an egg. Put a little bit of the hot squash in that bowl and stir quickly; add a little more hot squash so as to heat up the egg but not cook it. Add some real butter. Take about half a stack of saltines and crush them with your hands right into your bowl. Combine. Pour into a buttered casserole and bake at 350°F until bubbly. Sometimes I add some grated cheddar. Sometimes I top with buttered bread crumbs — panko, if I have it. Makes 4 generous servings.

There are jillions of squash casserole recipes. I like this one because it is how my mother made it, and the simplest version gives me the best squash flavor. My children like it best, too.

—Sue Paulsen, Clayton, Georgia

PUMPKIN YAMS

2 pounds fresh yams, steam-cooked until tender (let cool down after cooking)
2 tablespoons brown sugar
5 eggs
5 tablespoons flour
1¾ teaspoons vanilla
2 teaspoons baking powder
1 stick sweet butter, melted
2 teaspoons pumpkin pie spice

Mix all ingredients together in a food processor. Turn into a greased baking dish.

Mix together and place on top:
¼ cup chopped walnuts
¼ cup oatmeal
3 tablespoons brown sugar
2 teaspoons melted sweet butter

Bake at 350°F for 45 minutes or until lightly browned.

—Debbie Sharp Loeb, Freehold, New Jersey

BEEF STEW WITH GUINNESS

Allow for about 8 ounces of lean beef and half a largish onion per person. The remaining ingredients are 'to taste.' I include some or all of the following:

butter
olive oil
flour
strong beef stock (½ pint per 3 pounds of beef)
Guinness (¾ pint)
thyme
1 teaspoon wine vinegar
1 teaspoon brown sugar
about 4 cloves garlic
bouquet garni
2 bay leaves
soy sauce (Japanese tamari is best)
mushroom ketchup
tomato puree

I also like to throw in some button mushrooms. Prepare stock. Cut beef into strips, roughly 1 inch by 3 inches. Melt butter and olive oil in pan; quickly brown meat. Set aside. Chop onion, garlic, and thyme and lightly fry in pan juices. Stir in sufficient flour to make a roux, then add the stock and beer. (At this stage I also add soy sauce, mushroom ketchup, and tomato puree. These are optional extras, mostly for color.) Alternate beef and onion layers in casserole and pour stock/beer mix over it. Add mushrooms, bouquet garni, bay leaves, wine vinegar, and sugar.

Cover casserole dish and cook in 325°F oven for two and a half hours. Let it "rest" overnight (for some reason this improves the flavor). This is a good time to check for seasoning.

Choose a garlic bread covering or mashed potato and put over the top of the stew. With the latter, I sometimes mix in either parsnip or celeriac. Beat in butter, cream, or olive oil (to taste). Sprinkle with marjoram and grated nutmeg. Put covered stew back in the oven at a slightly higher temperature for half an hour. If the mashed potato covering fails a visual inspection, a brief spell under a hot broiler will brown and crisp the top. Serve with vegetables of choice.

This is a simple dish which can either be slow cooked in Guinness or any other dark beer (stout in the United Kingdom; I sometimes use Mackesons).

—Gordon Boals, Somerset, New Jersey

VEGETARIAN DISHES

Mary: "Jeff, these recipe look fabulous. I need quantities for each ingredient, however. We're supposed to be as thorough and specific as possible. Thanks."

Jeff: "Sorry, Mary; not going to happen. These recipes are designed for the creative heart and not the cookbook-chemist. Try them out and see what works."

These dishes are to be served at room temperature as appetizers or side dish. I love eating them from the opened door of the fridge with a fork in my hand. They are great to have around, especially in the summer when you want a cold meal. They keep well throughout the week.

RICE SALAD

cooked rice
diced red bell pepper
peas
salt and pepper
vinegar and oil

Combine the ingredients and season to flavor.

And Chris says: *An American or Australian Chardonnay will complement this salad.*

CAPPONATA

olive oil
garlic
1 can diced tomatoes
eggplant, cubed
black olives
oregano
carrots
diced red bell pepper

In a pot, heat the oil and brown the garlic. I put as much as a whole head of garlic in this dish. The secret is to brown the garlic to bring out a "nutty" taste. Add the eggplant and tomatoes with the oregano to stew for about and hour. Add the black olive, the carrots, and the bell pepper to stew for another half hour. This dish is great served at room temperature.

And Chris says: *An Oregon Pinot Noir or French Beaujolais...can't go wrong.*

STUFFED MUSHROOMS

mushrooms
garlic
grated cheese
olive oil
bread crumbs

I use the larger Portobello mushroom, but any caps of mushroom can be used.

Chop the mushroom stems, add the slivered garlic and the cheese of your choice with some bread crumbs. I like the sharper cheeses for this one: Parmesan, Romano, feta, blue cheese. Drizzle the oil olive on the stuffed mushroom cap and broil until the mushroom is cooked.

And Chris says: *French red Bordeaux or an American Claret or "House Blend" red with a good percentage of Mourvedre in it. Take notes and try a different wine next time you serve this dish.*

FENNEL SALAD

fennel
olive oil
white wine or stock
carrots
dash of curry

In a skillet, heat the oil and add the thinly sliced fennel. Add the white wine or the stock to steam the fennel. It takes between 20-30 minutes. Add the carrots to cook for 10 minutes with the dash of curry. Serve at room temperature.

And Chris says: *An Australian Chardonnay or American Viognier works well here. (You can also use the same wine in the salad.)*

TUSCAN WHITE BEANS AND POTATOES WITH ROSEMARY

soft white beans
boiled diced potato
olive oil
finely chopped rosemary

Cook the beans until soft. Add the diced potato. Dress with oil and finely chopped rosemary.

And Chris says: *Try a Washington State Riesling with this dish.*

POTATO FRITTERS WITH ONION AND CHEESE

mashed potato
diced onion
grated cheese
egg
bread crumbs

Mash the boiled potato with a little milk. Add the raw onion and the cheese of your choice. Form round balls. Dip them in egg, then bread crumbs, and quickly fry until crisp. These are better at room temperature than served hot.

And Chris says: *In the winter try an American Pinot Noir. In the summertime, light beer.*

LA-DE-DAH COLE SLAW WITH TRUFFLE OIL

sliced red cabbage
sliced red pepper
sliced onion
dill
caraway seed
white balsamic
truffle oil

Combine the ingredients. The salad is best when you let it sit at room temperature for at least an hour.

And Chris says: *French white Bordeaux or Chablis.*

ITALIAN GREENS

greens (rapini, collards, mustards)
stock
olive oil
garlic
red pepper flakes

In a pot, heat the oil and toast the garlic, then add the pepper flakes. Place the greens in the pot and add the stock.

And Chris says: *Try a well-chilled Italian Pinot Grigio.*

ZUCCHINI AND ONION

stock
onion
zucchini or summer squash
oregano
canned diced tomato

Combine the ingredients. Heat.

And Chris says: *American Viognier or New World Chardonnay.*

—Jeffrey Deutsch, St. Louis, Missouri

SAUCES, DRESSINGS,
SNACKS & BEVERAGES

CILANTRO-LIME SALAD DRESSING

In a blender, combine the following:

1 cup cilantro leaves, major stems removed

2 tablespoons red wine vinegar (no substitutions, please)

1 tablespoon fresh lime juice

1 tablespoon garlic, minced

1 tablespoon red onion, finely chopped

1 tablespoon honey

Begin to blend; pour in ½ cup olive oil while blending. Add salt and pepper to taste. Will keep up to a week in a sealed jar in the refrigerator.

—Lynn Ronkainen, Houston, Texas

VINAIGRETTE

1 cup olive oil

¼ cup vinegar (white wine, red wine, balsamic, whatever)

1 teaspoon Dijon mustard

¾ teaspoon salt

¼ teaspoon pepper

garlic to taste (optional)

Combine all ingredients.

—Alice Downs, Atlantic Highlands, New Jersey

EASY FRENCH DRESSING

Mix equal amounts of the following and shake well:

ketchup
sugar
oil
vinegar

This recipe sounds ridiculously easy and it is! It is a favorite in our family and everyone I serve it to loves it.

—Marcia Walker, Union Bridge, Maryland

EGG NOG (MRS. SEYMOUR'S RECIPE)

1 cup cream
2 cups milk
2 eggs
¼ cup sugar
1 cup whiskey
pinch of salt

Beat eggs; add sugar and beat until frothy and sugar has dissolved. Add the remaining ingredients, stirring thoroughly. Refrigerate over night. Yields 1 quart. Can easily be doubled, tripled, or quadrupled.

This is beguilingly smooth, delicious, expensive, and filled with calories. My mother, Mrs. Seymour, served this in small cups; it's stronger than it seems to be and will last longer that way.

—Sister Mary Elizabeth, Community of the Holy Spirit, New York, New York

CRANBERRY SAUCE

1 bag cranberries
2 cups water
1 cup sugar
2 packages lemon gelatin
1 cup chopped walnuts
1 cup chopped red grapes

Mix cranberries, water, and sugar in a saucepan. Bring to a boil and cook at a boil for 5 minutes (this makes the cranberries pop!). Add gelatin and mix well. Cool, then add the walnuts and grapes. Mix well, pour into a glass container, and refrigerate at least 8 hours.

As long as I can remember, my mother made this for Thanksgiving and Christmas. As a kid, I refused to eat it because I was "stoopid," but now I are smart and I eat this up, sometimes all on its lonesome! It deserves to be trotted out more than twice a year.

—Melissa Crandall Everett, Quaker Hill, Connecticut

SALUDA SALAD SPRINKLES

1 cup pumpkin seeds
½ cup sunflower seeds
¼ cup sesame seeds
¼-⅓ cup brewer's yeast
enough tamari or soy sauce to moisten

Preheat oven to 325°F. Mix all of the seeds and yeast together, then add the tamari or soy sauce until just moist. Mix well. Spread on a cookie sheet and bake for 15 minutes. Allow to cool on a cooling rack, then break up onto salad or enjoy for a snack. Store in an airtight container.

—The Rev. Gena D. Adams-Riley, Pensacola, Florida

MOM'S CAMPING MARINADE

Combine:

3 glugs* soy sauce
1 glug red wine vinegar
1 glug Worcestershire sauce
1 glug olive oil
A generous amount of dried thyme, plus some oregano and garlic powder to taste

*A glug can be anything; I use an ounce, but for bigger quantities of meat a glug could be ¼ cup or more.

This is good for chicken, pork chops, anything you like to marinate. Mother, who originated this recipe, was a gently raised New Jersey girl from Upper Montclair. She was not an enthusiastic camper, but she was an incredible chef. She would throw this marinade together and place it in a plastic bag with the chicken or whatever for a few hours in our cooler for our evening campout dinner. My sister says her husband married her because of this marinade.

—Cornelia (Corry) Weierbach, Arlington, Virginia

GARLICKY-CRANBERRY CHUTNEY

1-inch piece of ginger, peeled and cut into very thin slices
3-5 cloves garlic, finely chopped
½ cup cider vinegar
¼ cup sugar
⅛ teaspoon cayenne pepper
1 can whole-berry cranberry sauce
kosher salt
fresh ground pepper

Bring ginger, garlic, vinegar, sugar, and cayenne pepper to simmer in a small saucepan. Cook over medium heat until liquid is reduced to a cup, about 15 minutes. Add cranberry sauce and salt and pepper to taste. Mix and return to simmer. Cook on low heat for 10 minutes. Put in jars and refrigerate. Best when chilled overnight.

A sure thing for reducing leftovers!

—The Rev. Verne Woodlief, Whittier, California

FRESH 'N EASY BERRY JAM

2 envelopes unflavored gelatin
1 cup cold water
2 pints strawberries, sliced, and/or blueberries (about 4½ cups)
½ cup sugar (use more or less according to the ripeness of the fruit)
¼ cup lemon juice
2 to 3 tablespoons raspberry or orange liqueur (optional; I use 2 tablespoons Grand Marnier)

In a large saucepan, sprinkle unflavored gelatin over the cold water and let stand 1 minute. Stir over low heat until gelatin is completely dissolved, about 5 minutes. Add the fruit, sugar, and lemon juice. Bring to a boil, then simmer, stirring occasionally and crushing berries slightly, for 10 minutes. Stir in the liqueur. Spoon into jars; cool slightly before refrigerating. Chill until set, about 3 hours. Store up to 4 weeks in the refrigerator or up to 1 year in the freezer. Makes 4 cups of jam.

—Debbie Sharp Loeb, Freehold, New Jersey

APPETIZERS

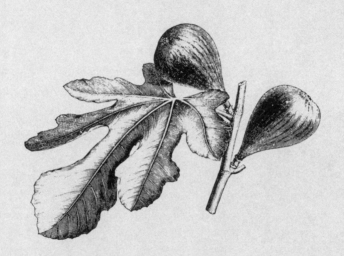

THEN THE IMAM FAINTED

The long season of rain in June seems to have slowed things down in the garden — for weeks, we have had an abundance of green tomatoes and not a single red one, long after the time when we would ordinarily be up to our necks in them. But Sunday, at last, the red avalanche began: the ruby globes peek from behind the leaves of every plant in the garden. And there are nineteen tomato plants this year, a fair number for two people.

But tomato gardening was never meant to be solely for the benefit of one's own household. Clearly, such a handsome fruit was meant to be shared. Q will dispense tomatoes to the neighbors, to our children, to the sexton of our old church, who looked forward to them every year and whom we still love. He'll give them, also, to people who just look to him like they need tomatoes.

Harvested food, in scripture, is meant to give away. After the farmer has harvested his crops, he is to leave some for the poor to gather. They come into the fields after the workers have left, and what remains is theirs for the taking.

City Harvest in New York does that with restaurants. They pick up in a truck what the restaurants don't sell, and bring it to food pantries and soup kitchens. Our guests at the pantry at St. Clement's sometimes had a City Harvest windfall: trays of expensive hors d'ouevres, baskets of breakfast breads, platters of luncheon meats, fancy desserts. Amy's Bread did that too, for our pantry: on Friday, what Amy didn't sell could go to the food pantry, and someone would go across the street after hours and come back with one or two enormous black plastic bags, fragrant with the lovely loaves. On the day the World Trade Center was destroyed, a truck pulled up in front of the church: a complete meal, for a meeting there that would never take place.

Tomatoes. Fresh in Q's lunchtime salad. Sliced on a plate at dinner. Fried in the morning for breakfast. Chopped and baked with chunks of eggplant and garlic and olive oil in one of his favorite Turkish dishes:

One day an imam was riding from one little town to another. He stopped at the home of a poor family on his way, and asked to be given something to eat. The wife of the house, honored to have the imam as her guest, set before him all the food they had, and her husband sat with him as he ate. One dish in particular was her pride and joy, the best thing she knew how to make. She watched anxiously as the imam picked up a piece of pita bread and dipped it into the dish. Would he like it? He tasted, and everyone was silent. He rolled his eyes toward heaven in delight and said, "Allah is great!" and fell over in a dead faint.

The name of the dish in Turkish is *Imam Byaldi*, which means *then the imam fainted.*

THEN THE IMAM FAINTED

Take as many tomatoes as you have and cut them into chunks. Take as many eggplants as you have and do the same. There should be slightly more eggplant than tomato. Put these into a greased, ovenproof dish. Mince 20 cloves of garlic and stir into the eggplant/tomato mixture. Add as much olive oil as you want and stir it in. Maybe 1/2 cup. Maybe less. Add pignoli nuts if you have them. Maybe 1/2 cup. Bake at 325°F for about an hour and a half, covered. Stir once or twice, if you want to. Eat it, hot or cold — sitting down — on pieces of pita.

—Barbara Cawthorne Crafton, The Geranium Farm

CURRIED OLIVE SPREAD

1 block of cream cheese (can be light cream cheese, if you're watching calories)
1 cup of pitted, chopped green salad olives (more or less to taste, and you can use other exotic olives if you so desire)
1 tablespoon curry (more or less to taste)

Cube the cream cheese, then put cheese and olives in a food processor. Blend until mixture is slightly lumpy. Stir in curry. Can be served immediately, but sitting in the fridge for an hour or so allows the flavors to blend. Serve with crackers, celery sticks, or toasted bread squares.

My grandmother gave me this recipe when I entered the working world. She told me there would be many occasions where I would be expected to bring an appetizer to a dinner, and this one was quick, easy, and tasted delicious. After all, she mused, working women were busy and didn't have all day to create fabulous food. It also works well with loose amounts and personal taste, important for those of us who fancy ourselves more artistic in the kitchen than we truly are.

As a priest, this spread has shown up at many a social event. After all, priests are busy and don't have all day to create fabulous food. So thanks to my grandmother, I can do it in less than 20 minutes.

—The Rev. Laurie Brock, Mobile, Alabama

SPINACH–ARTICHOKE DIP

2 10-ounce packages frozen chopped spinach
1 14-ounce can artichoke hearts, drained and chopped
1 10-ounce can fat-free mushroom soup, undiluted
1 8-ounce container reduced-fat sour cream
3 green onions, chopped
2 tablespoons all-purpose flour
1 tablespoon minced fresh parsley
¼ teaspoon Worcestershire
1 tablespoon butter
1 cup sliced fresh mushrooms
2 pressed garlic cloves
1 tablespoon lemon juice
½ teaspoon pepper
2 cups shredded Monterey Jack cheese, divided

Thaw and drain spinach well, squeezing out all water. Stir spinach with next 7 ingredients. Melt butter and cook mushrooms and next 3 ingredients; sauté 5 minutes. Stir mushroom soup mixture and 1 cup cheese into spinach mixture; spoon into a 7x11-inch baking dish or divide into 2 smaller dishes. Sprinkle with remaining cup of cheese. Bake at 400°F for 30 minutes.

—Lynda Creed, Pensacola, Florida

PIZZA ON THE BARBECUE

1 cup spreadable cream cheese
10-12 fresh chives, chopped
4-6 sundried tomatoes, marinated in olive oil
1-2 cloves garlic, chopped
1 medium pizza shell, pre-cooked

Empty cream cheese into medium bowl; stir to soften. Chop chives into small pieces and add to cream cheese. Cut sundried tomatoes into small pieces; add to cheese mixture. Press garlic; add to cheese mixture. Stir well.

Spread cheese mixture generously over surface of the pizza shell, then place shell directly onto heated barbeque grill. Heat pizza until cheese begins to melt. Slide pizza onto warm metal tray; cut into small pieces and serve. This is an excellent appetizer!

With long winters in southwestern Ontario, Canada, our family makes the most of summer hours. Barbecue meals are frequent and we look forward to the taste of grilled food. Pizza on the Barbeque adds another option to our list of favorite foods to grill. The chives are a tasty addition to the cream cheese, extra-welcome as they are grown in our garden. A small array of garden herbs is a tradition cultivated in our family. Enjoy!

—Patricia A. McGoldrick, Kitchener, Ontario, Canada

CALIFORNIA MYSTERY

1 cup mayonnaise
1 cup grated Swiss cheese
1 cup chopped red onion

Mix ingredients. Put in small Pyrex casserole dish. Bake at 350°F for 20-30 minutes or until bubbly and brown on top. Serve hot with sesame crackers.

—Dottie Pratt, Frederick, Maryland

THE WORLD'S BEST GUACAMOLE

4 ripe avocadoes
juice of 2 limes (fresh is best, not bottled)
6 green onions, chopped thin
2 small tomatoes, diced
1 garlic glove, smashed
drop of tequila
½ cup cilantro, finely chopped
½ cup green salsa
½ teaspoon ground roasted cumin
salt and fresh ground pepper to taste
½ teaspoon chili pepper
dash of Tabasco

Topping:
½ cup sour cream
½ cup grated cheddar cheese
½ cup pitted black olives, chopped

Scoop the avocadoes out of the shells, and discard the pits. Mash the avocadoes with a potato masher. Using a fork, whisk in the remaining ingredients. Place the guacamole in a medium serving dish.

Cover the entire surface with a layer of sour cream, so that there is no green showing. Sprinkle the grated cheese on top. Sprinkle on the olives. Cover the bowl with plastic wrap and refrigerate for at least 1 hour before serving. Serve with tortilla chips.

—Sharon Marable, Tuscaloosa, Alabama

CHICKEN NIBBLE

6 ounces frozen orange juice concentrate
2 tablespoons soy sauce
1 teaspoon celery seed
1 teaspoon minced ginger
½ teaspoon Tabasco
½ teaspoon salt
18 chicken wings

Thoroughly mix all ingredients except chicken wings. Cut each wing at each of the two joints. Use the two meaty sections; save the third for stock. Place wings, skin down, side-by-side in a shallow baking dish; cover with sauce.

Bake in at 350°F for 25 minutes; turn wings. Cook another 20 minutes or until tender and nicely colored. Serve hot or cold. Recipe may be increased to serve many by doubling or tripling.

I have been bringing this to receptions at Grace Episcopal Church for twenty years.

—Gary Carter, Alexandria, Virginia

MEEM'S PICKLED SHRIMP

2½ pounds shrimp
½ cup celery tops
1½ tablespoons sugar (you may omit if you are counting carbs)
1 cup mixed pickling spices (use ½ cup in cooking shrimp and ½ cup when
  warming vinegar)
2-3 large white onions
7-8 bay leaves
1½ cups salad oil (canola is best)
¾ cup white vinegar
1½ teaspoons salt
2½ teaspoons capers, juice and all
dash of red pepper

Cook shrimp in ½ cup pickling spices. Peel shrimp and place in a container with lid. Add remaining ingredients, other than vinegar and ½ cup spice, to bowl. Boil vinegar and spices and pour over the mixture in the bowl. Stir and allow to cool. Place lid or plastic wrap over the top of the container and place in the refrigerator for 8 hours to 2 weeks. Be sure to use a glass container, high-quality plastic, or pottery to store the shrimp.

I make this over Thanksgiving weekend and serve it around the Christmas holidays. The only problem I have with this time frame is my family tasting it to see how it is coming along! My family eats everything from the dish on crackers. I sometimes add more shrimp to the mix if the numbers deplete too quickly; when I do this I do not reheat the vinegar.

—Sarah Moden-Alliston, Pound Ridge, New York

BREAD, BREAKFAST & BRUNCH

DAD'S WHOLE WHEAT DOUGH BREAD

Yield: 2 loaves
Details: 2 greased 8$\frac{1}{2}$x4$\frac{1}{2}$x2$\frac{1}{2}$-inch loaf pans
3$\frac{3}{4}$ hours rising time, total
375°F
15 minutes plus 45 minutes baking time

1 package active dry yeast or 1 cake compressed yeast
¼ cup water (warm, not hot)
2½ cups hot water (has to melt the shortening, margarine, or butter)
½ cup brown sugar
3 teaspoons salt
¼ cup shortening
3 cups stirred whole-wheat flour (any type will do, but I especially like stone-ground coarse whole wheat flour)
5 cups sifted all-purpose white flour (high-gluten bread flour is better, but use general purpose if that's what you've got)

Soften the yeast in the warm (not hot) water, 10 minutes or so. Combine the hot water, sugar, salt, and shortening, and cool until lukewarm. (Be patient! The biggest clues to bread-making are not too hot and take your sweet time.) Stir the whole wheat flour and 1 cup of white flour into the milk, and beat them together well. Add the softened yeast to the flour, and mix them together. Add enough remaining flour to the dough to make it moderately stiff. (Add the flour gradually and work in each addition. Take your sweet time!)

Turn the dough out onto a lightly floured surface. Knead the dough until it's smooth and satiny, about 10-12 minutes. Shape the dough into a ball and place it in a lightly greased bowl, turning it once to grease its surface. Cover the bowl. Let the dough rise in a warm place until it's doubled, about 1$\frac{1}{2}$ hours.

Punch the dough down, and cut it into halves. Shape the halves into balls, cover them, and let them rest for 10 minutes. Shape the balls into loaves.

Place the halves in 2 greased loaf pans. Let the loaves rise until they've doubled, about 1$\frac{1}{4}$ hours. Bake the loaves in a moderate (375°F) oven for about 45 minutes, or until they're done. After 25 minutes, if the tops are browning too fast, cover them with aluminum foil.

—Chris Jones, Schenectady, New York

CAPE COD BANANA BREAD

Preheat oven to 350°F. Grease one large loaf pan, or two small loaf pans.

Mash together into a small bowl:
3 very ripe bananas
¼ cup vegetable oil
1 cup sugar
1 teaspoon vanilla

Sift together into a separate bowl:
2 cups flour
½ teaspoon baking powder
½ teaspoon baking soda
½ teaspoon salt

Add wet ingredients to dry and stir only until moist; about 20-30 strokes. Don't waste any time transferring the batter into the pan and right to the oven. Bake for 45 minutes or until golden brown and a knife or skewer inserted in the center comes out clean.

   Butter does make a rich addition to the batter in the place of oil, but is not necessary. We sometimes add chocolate chips, blueberries, or other fresh or dried fruit (a large handful of whatever happens to be on hand). Sometimes we add a dash or two of nutmeg, pumpkin pie spice, or cardamom if we are feeling spicy, especially in the fall.

I have been living with this recipe for over 16 years, which is just over half of my life. I know it like the back of my hand and everyone who I've shared the recipe with has thanked me numerous times. Yes, I hate to admit it; it's that good! My sons, ages 2 and 4, come running to help mash the bananas and about an hour later the 6-year-old neighbor boy comes running over for a slice, and one to take to his mom. We live on Cape Cod now and have many friends with little ones in school and just starting school. It's funny how everyone has someone in their classes who have food allergies. This recipe works for them very well. Other flours can even be substituted, with some experimenting, I imagine. Anyway, enjoy! I know I do!

—Barbara Hersey, Hyannis, Massachusetts

ANNA'S BUBBIE'S MANDEL BREAD

2 eggs, well beaten
¾ cup sugar
juice and rind of ½ lemon
½ teaspoon vanilla
2⅓ cups flour
¼ cup oil
¼ cup chopped almonds
2 teaspoons baking powder

Preheat oven to 325°F. Beat eggs; add sugar and beat together. Add lemon, vanilla, and 1 cup of flour; mix well. Add almonds and oil; mix well. Add remaining flour and baking powder; mix well. Knead into 2 long loaves. (This is sticky dough!) Place on oiled and floured baking sheets, and bake for 20-30 minutes. Cut into slices while still warm, then return to oven to brown.

On the recipe card from Anna, she notes that her grandmother had written down "this recipe is from Arthur Siegel's mother in New Jersey, many, many years ago." Who's Arthur Siegel?

—Melissa Crandall Everett, Quaker Hill, Connecticut

SWEET POTATO BISCUITS {A MISSISSIPPI TREAT}

2 cups all-purpose flour
2 teaspoons baking powder
½ teaspoons soda
1 teaspoon sugar
1 teaspoon salt
¼ cup shortening
1 cup mashed baked sweet potato*
½ cup + 1 tablespoon buttermilk

*do not use canned sweet potato

Combine all dry ingredients; cut in shortening until mixture appears mealy. Mix potato and buttermilk together; stir into flour mixture. Put dough onto floured board and knead 5 or 6 strokes. Roll out to ½- to ¾-inch thick. Cut into rounds and place on lightly greased baking sheet. Bake at 400°F about 10 minutes. Serve hot with plenty of butter. (Unbaked biscuits may be frozen.) Makes about 2 dozen 2-inch biscuits.

—Jane Wacaster, Meridian, Mississippi

CHEDDAR APPLESAUCE MUFFINS

2 cups all-purpose baking mix
¼ cup sugar
1 teaspoon cinnamon
1 egg, well-beaten
½ cup unsweetened applesauce
½ cup skim milk
2 tablespoons oil
1 cup sharp cheddar cheese, shredded

Combine baking mix, sugar, and cinnamon. In separate bowl, combine egg, applesauce, milk, oil, and cheese. Add to dry ingredients; mix lightly. Spray muffin pan and fill each cup two-thirds full. Bake at 400°F for 15-20 minutes. Makes 1 dozen.

—Rachael Taylor, Andalusia, Alabama

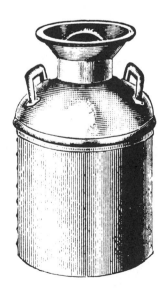

EGGS WITH A HAT {A.K.A. TOAD IN THE HOLE}

1 slice bread
1 egg
margarine
cheese (optional)

Use a glass or biscuit cutter and cut a hole in the center of the bread. Melt some margarine in a pan. Put slices of bread in the pan. Put the holes in, too. Break an egg into the holes in the bread. Cook until the eggs are done and the cut-out holes are browned. Optional: put a slice of cheese over each piece of bread and melt, and then put the "hat" back on.

This can also be served with salsa. My grandsons like salsa, so we add that. When my girls were small this was the best! For fun, you can cut the bread out with different shaped cookie cutters. Then, of course, there is always green eggs and ham!

—Sally Tarasoff, Boerne, Texas

SCRAPPLE

¾-pound sausage
1 cup water
1 cup evaporated milk
½ cup cornmeal
½ cup evaporated milk
¼ teaspoon salt
¼ teaspoon black pepper
drained fat from sausage

Scramble, fry, and drain sausage. Bring the water and 1 cup evaporated milk to boil in large pan. Moisten cornmeal with 1/2 cup evaporated milk. Add salt and pepper. Quickly stir until liquid boils. Cover and lower heat to medium. Cook 5 minutes, stirring occasionally, removing from heat each time for safety from popping mixture. Stir in sausage and pour into wet loaf pan. Cover and chill overnight.

To serve, slice and roll slices in flour. Fry in the drained sausage fat (now we health-conscious would use olive oil!) until crispy-crusted like potato cakes. Serves 4-6. Serve with stewed apples and/or maple syrup.

This was a family Christmas morning tradition in our family as I was growing up. Make a day or two ahead so there is little fuss on a busy morning!

—The Rev. B. Chari Mynatt, Lee's Summit, Missouri

BREAD FOR THE WORLD

My first baking with yeast took place when I was about fifteen. I was alone in the kitchen — my mother did not bake with yeast, and both my grandmothers were dead: there was nobody to tell me how. Hot Cross Buns was what I was going to make, and I knew what they would be like: tall and fragrant, studded with raisins and tiny bits of peel. Something went wrong, though — even now, I cannot say what it was. The buns were not tall and light. They were small and leaden, as flat as hockey pucks. I sighed and painted a white icing cross on each one anyway, and my father said they were very good. Nice and chewy. He was a fine man.

That was long ago. Today my rolls balloon to the proper volume without even being asked, and they are mildly famous in my family, to the extent that major feasts are not considered complete without them. The living yeast fascinates me still, though, all the more now that I know how to manage it.

Crumble it into a cup of warm water and stir a little: within minutes, it has begun to breathe, to swell, to soften and come to life in its medium of warm water. Little plant spores, that's what yeast is: waiting in their package until you come along with warmth and water and remind it that it's alive. Mixed with the flour, it begins to feed on it as well, growing and swelling still more, so that when you come back to the bowl in which you left it a couple of hours ago, it has become a gorgeous dome, rising right out of the bowl. Punch it down, in an unforgettable moment of childish fun, and the legacy of its swelling is everywhere in its texture: elastic, smooth, irresistible. And then form it into loaves and leave it alone and it swells again, even more this time, twice as fast. Nothing can stop it.

Except that's not all there is to it. In order for there to be bread, the yeast must die.

In every place where a microscopic yeast spore balloons to many times its own size there will be a pocket of air, left there by its death. A yeast-shaped hole. A bread oven is hot — 450 or 500 degrees Fahrenheit. The yeast spores do not survive it. They give their lives for the loaf of bread.

And yet their memory is everywhere in the loaf. They shaped it. Their bodies gave it the power to rise. You even taste and smell them, still, though they are gone: their warm malty flavor is what makes yeast bread different from other bread — from crackers, or biscuits, or muffins.

This is my body, given for you. It cannot be at all unless I give my life for it. You are the body. You and me and the bread, we are body together. And I am in you, and you in me.

—Barbara Cawthorne Crafton,
The Geranium Farm

CORN SPOON BREAD

1 cup milk
1 tablespoon butter
1 cup cornmeal
1 can creamed corn
2 eggs, separated
1 tablespoon salt
1 tablespoon pepper

Scald the milk in a saucepan. Melt the butter into the milk. Add the cornmeal and cook until thick. Stir in the creamed corn. Beat the egg yolks with the salt and pepper. Stir the yolks into the corn mixture. Beat the egg whites to stiff peaks. Fold the egg whites into the corn mixture. Pour into a well-greased quart baking dish. Bake at 350°F for 50 minutes to 1 hour or until a wooden skewer inserted in the middle comes out clean. Serves 6-8.

This is a favorite recipe of mine from my Indiana childhood.

—The Rev. Gerald W. Keucher, New York, New York

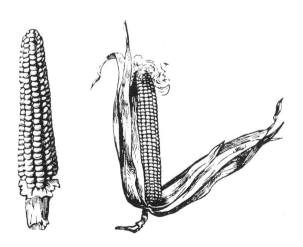

TASTE AND SEE THAT THE LORD IS GOOD EUCHARISTIC BREAD

1 package dry yeast (2½ teaspoons if you buy it in bulk)
½ cup warm water
1 teaspoon sugar

Dissolve the sugar and yeast in the warm water in a small bowl and let it proof somewhere warm. (My gas oven set on OFF, warmed only by the pilot light, is perfect for this.)

Meanwhile, combine in a large bowl:
1 tablespoon salt
3 tablespoons olive oil (extra virgin is best)
4 tablespoons honey
1½ cups warm water
1½ cups white flour

Stir vigorously with a whisk until smooth. Add the yeast mixture (which should be foamy by now) and stir well. To this, add enough whole wheat flour to make a dough firm enough to pull cleanly away from the sides of the bowl when stirred vigorously. Usually 2½ cups but sometimes more, sometimes less. Turn the dough out onto a floured board and let it rest for about 10 minutes. (Ignore this rest at your peril! Bread dough needs a Sabbath rest as much as its maker does.) Knead the dough, adding flour as needed, until it's smooth and elastic. Wash and lightly oil the bowl in which you made it, return the dough to the bowl, cover it with plastic wrap, and let it rise in a warm place until doubled in bulk.

Pre-heat oven to 350°F. Punch down dough and turn it out onto a lightly floured board. Cut into 8 equal pieces. With floured hands, shape each piece into a disc, and place onto oiled cookie sheet. Slash a cross onto the top of each disk with a razor blade or sharp knife, and bake immediately for 12-15 minutes (depending on your oven). When cool, double-wrap. It freezes well, and like any bread, should be thawed in its wrappers at room temperature. Makes 8 Eucharistic breads.

This makes 8 slightly sweet, intensely flavorful Eucharistic loaves that if properly made will be moist and dense, but not heavy. It breaks into small pieces easily for distribution and stands up to intinction without crumbling. One loaf will feed approximately 50 communicants, and you will have small children and grown men ask you afterwards if there is any left over. It takes approximately 4 hours from start to finish, but you are actually touching the ingredients and the dough for only about 10 minutes of that time. The rest is spent waiting and if you're like me, you'll want to steward it wisely. So give yourself a pedicure, pray the Daily Office, read a story to your daughter, brush the cat, answer your e-mail.

—The Rev. Susan Sommer, New Lenox, Illinois

EASY BREAD

Mix:
3 cups flour
½ cup sugar
dash of salt

Add:
6 large teaspoons of shortening (I like the butter-flavored stuff)

Mix with a fork until crumbly.

Dissolve:
2 teaspoons yeast in 2 cups warm water

Add to mixture. Add **3 more cups flour.**

Mix and knead on floured surface adding flour until it is not tacky. Then, knead until rubbery. Shape into balls about 3 inches across or braid into 2 loaves. Cut tops of rolls in cross design or parallel lines. Bake at 350°F about 30 minutes. Eating a roll is the best way to know if it is done. You'll get the hang of it after a while. This bread is not light and fluffy. It is solid and wholesome. Makes 3 dozen rolls or 2 loaves.

I used to make this bread for a friend who catered in Austin, Texas. It traveled well, had a nice yeast flavor, and was used on buffet tables with fruit and cheese. I usually mixed grains and bran and stuff to make it hippie — I mean, healthy!

—Suzanne Armstrong, San Antonio, Texas

HONEY GRANOLA

2 cups regular (not quick-cooking) rolled oats
2 tablespoons light brown sugar
¼ teaspoon ground cinnamon
1 cup slivered almonds
1 cup unsalted sunflower seeds (or you can substitute 2 cups of any kind of chopped nuts)
4 tablespoons (½ stick) unsalted butter
¼ cup honey

Preheat oven to 325°F. Lightly spray a baking sheet (with sides) with cooking spray. Combine oats, sugar, cinnamon, and nuts, toss well to mix. Melt butter and honey in a small saucepan; do not boil. Stir to mix. Immediately pour over oat mixture and stir to blend all ingredients. Spread onto baking sheet; bake until golden, about 25-30 minutes. Cool to room temperature in pan. Do not stir. With a spatula remove from pan "in chunks" and store at room temperature.

Note: If you double the recipe, use a 12x13-inch pan. I always double, because it is so good! Use with yogurt, fruit, ice cream, as a snack, anytime!

This is one of those "if-you-could-only-take-one-thing-to-eat-on-an-island" recipes. Healthful, goes on all kinds of good stuff, from yogurt to fruit to ice cream to a pile of M&M's when you have a chocolate attack. I keep a huge jar of it on my kitchen counter at all times. Not only for myself, but those times when someone does something nice, and you want to say "thanks."

—The Rev. Virginia Hill Monroe, Cashiers, North Carolina

PARMESAN CHEESE GRITS

1 cup stone ground grits or just "plain old grits"
2 cups chicken stock
1 cup of water
1 dash of olive oil
salt for the water
1 roasted onion (roasted on the grill, if you can)
1 cup whole cream
3 ounces evaporated milk
1 can cream of celery soup
1 cup grated Parmesan cheese
basil leaves

Put onion on grill to roast. After several minutes on the grill to release the flavors, add it to a small sauce pan with the whole cream and evaporated milk. Let them sit and rest until time to add to grits. Bring water and chicken stock to a boil. Add dash of olive oil and salt. Pour in grits and onion and cook until done. Add celery soup and mix until smooth. Remove the onion from the milk mixture and save the onion for garnish. Slowly begin to add the cream mixture to the grits. Add Parmesan cheese and continue to mix until very smooth. Place in casserole dish. Chop roasted onion and spread on top and then garnish with basil leaves. Serve warm to hot. Serves 6-8.

This is the greatest grits dish I've ever eaten, and living in the South, that is something!

—Handy Avery, Huntsville, Alabama

HASH BROWN BREAKFAST CASSEROLE

8 ounces frozen, shredded hash brown potatoes
8 ounces Velveeta cheese cubes
8 ounces shredded Cheddar cheese
1 can cream of celery soup
1 pound lean sausage
¼ cup diced onions
3 eggs
1½ (10.75-ounce) soup cans of milk
salt and pepper to taste

Brown the sausage (hot or regular style) and onion. Drain off any grease. In a large bowl, mix eggs, milk, celery soup, and cheeses. Add potatoes and browned sausage. Blend together well and pour into a 9x13-inch glass baking dish. Bake at 375°F for approximately 45 minutes or until bubbling and lightly browned on top. Casserole can be made ahead of time or overnight. For added flavor, serve with salsa or picante sauce. Approximately 8-10 servings.

—Louise Lane, Limon, Colorado

CHEESY OLIVE BREAD

½ cup mayonnaise
1 cup ripe olives, chopped
2 cloves garlic, minced
½ cup butter, softened
2 cups mozzarella cheese, grated
6 green onions, chopped
3 loaves French bread

Cut French bread in half lengthwise. Cream butter and mayonnaise; add remaining ingredients and spread on each half of bread. Bake uncovered at 350°F until cheese is fully melted. One recipe will make approximately 20 slices, depending on thickness of the slices.

This recipe was given to Mary Weems from Nancy Rey, both teachers at Meridian Public Schools and natives of this wonderful Mississippi town. Please remember us when you are enjoying this! Bon appetit!

—Mary Weems and Nancy Rey, Meridian, Mississippi

CHEESY SALLY LUNN BREAD

1 cup milk
1 tablespoon salt
½ cup butter
⅓ cup sugar
1 package dry yeast
2 tablespoons warm water
4 eggs, well-beaten
1 tablespoon coarsely-cracked fresh pepper
1 heaping cup sharp cheddar cheese, grated
4½ cups flour

Heat the milk and butter in a saucepan with the sugar, stirring to dissolve. Remove from the heat and cool to lukewarm. After softening the yeast in the water, add the yeast to the mixture. Set aside until bubbly.

Turn mixture into a bowl and add beaten eggs, flour, and salt; add cheeses and pepper. Beat well, about 500 strokes by hand. If you use a food processor, the dough should be smooth, shiny, and not too sticky (it will be soft, however). Cover and let rise until doubled in size, about an hour. Beat down and turn into a greased 9-inch diameter tube pan. Let rise again for about an hour or until doubled.

Bake in a 375°F preheated oven for about 40 minutes or until golden. Let rest a few minutes, then turn pan upside down and remove bread to complete cooling.

Yield: one large loaf; about 15 slices.

—Gary Carter, Alexandria, Virginia

SWEDISH CHEESE PITA

2 tablespoons flour
1 container cottage cheese
½ stick butter, cut up
3 eggs
½ package frozen spinach, thawed, and water pressed out in a sieve
8 slices sharp cheddar cheese

Preheat oven to 350°F. Combine all ingredients. Put in a greased 9-inch non-metal pan. Bake for 1 hour. Cool 10 minutes before serving.

It's incredibly easy and not even bad for you, according to some new diet principles. Of course, you can use low-fat cottage cheese and 2% cheese, if you really must. I mostly double it and serve it for brunch with a tomato aspic salad, which you unmold during the 10 minutes the thing needs to set up after cooking. This provides a no-effort, high-effect ladies' luncheon! Raves guaranteed!

—Virginia Benson, St. Louis, Missouri

INDEX